THE O
MELCHIZEDEK

IAN CLAYTON

Produced by Revelation Partners
with grateful thanks to our wonderful international
transcription and editing team who wish
to remain anonymous

Ian Clayton: www.sonofthunder.org

Produced with help from our wonderful volunteer team of Kingdom warriors by Revelation Partners: www.revelationpartners.org

Published by Son of Thunder Publications:
www.sonofthunderpublications.org

Fine art for cover design hand painted
by Kim Dokka www.kimdokka.com

Cover Design by Aspect Reference Design:
Caleb.gabrial@clear.net.nz

Each chapter in this book is an edited and updated transcript taken from messages given by Ian Clayton at different times over a several year period.

There are some minor differences from the audio messages the reader might have listened to before.

ISBN 978-1-911251-08-8

Graphic support Iain Gutteridge www.ig-graphic-design.co.uk

Typeset by Avocet Typeset, Somerton, Somerset, TA11 6RT

Printed in the United Kingdom

For Worldwide Distribution

Contents

ACKNOWLEDGEMENTS

Partnering with Ian Clayton to write this new volume of his revelatory teaching has been an honour and a privilege. Thank You Abba, Your ongoing commission to see these books written has been a strength and an inspiration to us, with visionary experiences of arenas of heaven and the angelic amid the battles. Recording prophecy and inspirational teaching has always been our heart passion, but there has never been a speaker whose words have inspired us in the creation of a book until Ian Clayton came to the UK a number of years ago. Our greatest goal in seeing Ian Clayton's work published, is to unlock the experience of being in heavenly realms with Christ for those wanting to find this reality.

We want to honour the support, friendship and dedication of our IT and media team and the many others whose attention and diligence have been invaluable, together with the graphic design expertise of several talented team members, especially our design lead Gabrial Heath of Aspect Reference Design, who created the cover for us and Iain Gutteridge for his excellent graphic support throughout. We owe special gratitude to our media and IT support team, including Andy Page who created the YouTube video, Prav Kumar who created much of the website and our spectacular project manager and 'go to guy' who wishes to remain anonymous.

We want to especially thank all the Kingdom family in Christ who donated to help with the creation and publication costs of this book. We couldn't have done it without your touching generosity and we were moved and encouraged by all the wonderful messages of support, thank you so much.

Our special thanks goes to our wonderful, international transcription team, whose generous and loving companionship on the journey brought about the birth of this new book months before it might otherwise have been available. Thank you so much, all of you, our friends named and those wishing to remain anonymous. May the Lord pour the blessing your work gives to others into your hearts and lives as well.

We cannot give adequate thanks to the numerous precious sisters and several dedicated brothers who walked with us along the journey of creating this book, including proof readers, intercessors and friends of wise counsel, without whom this book would still be a vision. They have chosen to remain anonymous but they continue to be counted with affection as part of the Revelation Partners family.

We also want to express our love and gratitude for the kindness, encouragement and prayer of many which opened doors along the way, including Stephen McKie of Scotland Ablaze; Matthew and Pearl Nagy of Glory Company and the wonderful Kingdom family in Horsham; Liz Wright, Lulu, Ann, Anne, Funmi and precious prayer community in Guildford and faithful intercessors and friends Michelle Beare and Michelle Kerslake – thank you so much for your loving support for this work as we walk into heavenly realms together.

We would like to express our heartfelt thanks and appreciation to Carole Carrick and the team of volunteers who worked so tirelessly on this material.

Finally, we want to express our affection and gratitude to Ian, his wife, family and team, especially Karl Whitehead, for their wisdom, support and oversight of this labour of love.

Revelation Partners
United Kingdom
2017

RECOMMENDATIONS

Just when I believe my grid is filled to capacity with awesome revelations, I learn that my friend Ian is downloading amazing new stuff. Ian's incredible revelations have required me to obtain a new OS (operating system), coupled with next level storage capacity, designed to handle the weight of the new glory. I believe I know why Ian Clayton is gifted with amazing abilities to receive so many ancient treasures. It is not only because he is a man of honor and love for the Father YHVH, but because he engages with all his being what has been given to him. If we likewise dare to engage what Ian is downloading and revealing within the pages of this new book, we too will find more ancient paths and reveal dimensionally YHVH 's glory and majesty in all of creation. Love It!

Aaron Smith
The Rock of Mobile, Alabama U.S.A.
Author of "Come Up Here"

Ian Clayton's relationship with YHVH is revealed in the truth of the Kingdom that he brings forth. His heart to please YHVH is evident when he speaks, and is valuable in bringing many sons to maturity. The Order of Melchizedek is packed full of protocol, making plain the path that we who read may run with confidence. Ian is a man of honor and is fearless in mandating the mystical. The Order of Melchizedek leads us into the ever increasing Kingdom, from glory to glory.

Teresa Bowen
The Rock of Mobile, Alabama U.S.A.
Author of "Zadok The New Old Order"

Ian's new book is one we've been looking forward to with great anticipation and now it has materialized! "The Order of Melchizedek" is a timely release to those who are born from above and want to know what God has in store for us and to reveal our heavenly identity on earth. I believe this book will change the lives of many fellow believers and stir in us to walk in the newness of God.

Watchman Ngiam, Singapore

We were recently asked the question, "Who are some of the most significant individuals walking the earth today?" We said it would take a bit of time to come up with a list, but one name pops up immediately: Ian Clayton. Ian's extraordinary life and phenomenal teachings are a gift to our generation, bearing fruit that will remain forever.

Kings, Priests, Legislators, Oracles – that is who we are as heirs of God and joint-heirs with Jesus Christ.

Through the remarkable revelation that unfolds in the pages of this great book, Ian is awakening us to true sonship – the world-changing godliness and power within those who recognize their identity and arise to the responsibility YHWH has given us. Let's read it; let's assimilate the treasure found in this field; and let us continually be transformed by the renewing of our mind!

Marios and Danielle Ellinas
Connecticut, USA

Ian Clayton is a pursuer of "knowing Him" His encounter of coming to the knowledge of the true God started Him on the journey to be taught of Him through His word. He searches the deep things of God and desires others to know Him and the power of His resurrection. I love that he challenges every believer to know the Word and eagerly submits his doctrine. He is not just about seeking Him, but about manifesting Him through the fruits of the spirit and walking with character and discipline to honor the Father as well as his desire to see all sons walk as Yeshua walked.

It is a delight to call him my friend.

Peace
Michelle
Abundant Ministries
Yarash.org

I honour Ian for the past years of influence in my life and I thank him for his mentoring in understanding of the spiritual realms. Drawing us into the Fathers court room, teaching us protocols of the heavenly court system.

Ian has been a forerunner in this area and an influence in my life for the past seven years. I commend Ian and this new book to you.

It contains many new truths that follow on from the teaching in his previous two books.

Mrs Jane Schroeder
fierycrownandglory.com

Statement of Faith

As YHVH leads us from one degree of glory to another we have to humbly accept that we may not believe today everything that we believed yesterday and tomorrow may bring yet more mysteries and treasures of glory that the Father has kept for us in the dark cloud of His presence until such a day as this. But the Word of the Lord remains and with it some pillars of truth I want to share with you as a guide while you take the journey in this book with me.

We believe:

That the Torah, Tanakh (Old Testament) and the New Testament Bible are the only infallible record of the Word of God and need to be honoured in that way.

That Yeshua is the actual Son of God, He was born of a virgin, came to earth fully man, fully God.

That Yeshua died and was raised to life from the grave to show us a way into our future.

That the blood of Yeshua is the most powerful instrument given to us as believers to empower us to become transformed to bear His (Yeshua's) image on the earth here.

The transfiguring of Christ on the mountain was revealed to us and will reveal us in that glory.

Christ's death on the cross and resurrection from the grave are fully embraced by my ministry body.

We believe in a mystery that no eye has seen and no ear heard which is stored up for those that believe. Things that are not yet known by man that YHVH will unlock in the future as part of the inheritance for the sons of God and we really believe that there are things that have not been done or seen on the earth. We will hopefully in this book be picking some of those things up and starting to walk with you through the process of maturity to handle the responsibilities of the mysteries that YHVH has given to us to steward in creation.

We measure everything against the nine plumb lines of belief systems:

Righteousness, joy and peace
The way the truth and the life
Judgment, justice and holiness

Those nine strings we weigh against every encounter and we do that on purpose so that there is a common goal, purpose and image behind everything that we do, so that even if we have some unexpected experiences we can judge it all by those nine strings and if there is one string missing then it needs to be looked at seriously and put aside until you get further revelation on it or left to go onto something else.

Ian Clayton
New Zealand 2017

CHAPTER 1
DEVELOPING YOUR CHARACTER

Introduction – our maturity as sons

I believe that YHVH is establishing something on the face of the earth called the Order of Melchizedek. *"For he testifies, You are a priest forever after the order of Melchizedek"* (Hebrews 7:17). I want to look at the outworking of this and unlock some of the protocol so you can begin to see that there is a hope beyond what we may presently understand as believers.

I believe we are now coming into the time when we. as sons, have the capacity to reach right into the realm of the future, live out of it and to, literally, be writing history. The whole issue of our identity is about our full maturity.

We need to realise that YHVH is looking for mature sons. He is looking for Lords and Kings. It is actually about being a mature son and the protocols of maturity as a son that validate your position in heaven. It has got nothing to do with your position on earth. The earth will respond to your position in heaven, but the earth will not respond to your position on the earth. That is why the earth has not changed, even though we have had apostles up to now because it has got nothing to do with the earth. The function of the five-fold ministry was put in place for the building of the body of Christ, for the maturing of the believers until that which is perfect has come. *"And he gave some, apostles; and some, prophets; and some, evangelists; and some, pastors and teachers; For the perfecting of the saints, for the work of the ministry, for the edifying of the body of Christ: Till we all come in the unity of the faith, and of the knowledge of the Son of God, unto a perfect man, unto the measure of the stature of the fullness of Christ"* (Ephesians 4:11-13 KJ2000). *"...But when that which is perfect has come, then that which is partial will pass away"* (1 Corinthians 13:10 TLV). I believe that the 'until' and the 'perfect' has now arrived and it is called the Order of Melchizedek. As sons who do what we see our Father doing as Christ did (John 5:19), we are becoming less dependent on spiritual gifts to teach each other because, since December 2012, YHVH has been establishing the age where, *"They shall not teach every man his neighbor, and every man his brother, saying, Know the Lord: for all shall know me, from the least to the greatest"* (Hebrews 8:11). This is a heavenly, governmental priesthood. An earthly, flaming engagement of a completely different tabernacle that is a reflection of heaven on earth, not of earth trying to get into heaven. I really do believe that this order is very misunderstood as there is very little known about it.

I had my very first encounter with Melchizedek almost ten years ago when the Lord began to speak to me about honouring the vessel which is all about silver. I was in a meeting where people had traded a hundred and eighty collectable silver coins into the offering. The next day we had about thirty gold coins put into the offering. YHVH had opened up a door because of an encounter He was trying to speak to me about at that time. In fact, 2013 was the ten year anniversary of that door opening. Then I had an encounter with Melchizedek when I was in the treasury room in heaven. Melchizedek said to me, "It is all yours, Ian!" I had no idea how to handle the resource of wealth at *that* stage, but YHVH's desire is to mature us into responsibility. *"The blessing of the LORD, it makes rich, and he adds no sorrow with it"* (Proverbs 10:22). The function of a king is to have the riches to be able to dispense justice and bring mercy and grace to be able to help his people (Psalm 72).

In this book I will go through the meaning of the Order of Melchizedek and some of the things that are associated with it. It is very important that you recognise when revelation about this order starts to unfold in the atmosphere. The presence of YHVH witnesses and testifies to it. Part of our functionality in this order is our role as a priest. In the following chapters, I am going to lay out some foundation for what YHVH needs to do inside of you to bring you into that place and its function and role. I remember the powerful encounter I had with Melchizedek the night I wrote my talk on The Law of Faith. The Law of Faith is central to our walk as sons in the Order of Melchizedek and we will be going on to look at that in the next chapter.

In this first chapter I want to lay some foundations, and throughout the book challenge the beliefs you may have inherited from the religious system that may not be right. We will examine some of the things we think we know, and things that have been established patterns inside our lives. We will then hopefully undo some of those processes which have proven unfruitful. My desire is to help you reach a completely different place in the spirit by the end of this book than you might feel in as you are now beginning this journey with me.

I believe YHVH is moving in the body of Christ in a new and completely different way today. I do not think that many of us yet have a perspective of how important we are in His purposes. There is an advancing Kingdom, and of that Kingdom there will be no end. *"There shall be no end to the increase of His government and of peace… over his kingdom"* (Isaiah 9:7 AMP). That Kingdom is being birthed in the earth, and its government is going to rest on the earth. The sons are going to find their seats (Ephesians 2:6), and they are going to be able to rule and have dominion over the earth *("I saw thrones on which were seated those who had been given authority to judge"* (Revelation 20:4). We need to realize who we really are. When we become born again, and the life of YHVH begins to flow through our life, we have the capacity to frame[1] our world.

But character is the crucible that is supposed to hold all of our spirituality, and travelling all over the world, I am seeing character failure in many churches and even some leaders.

Major flaws are showing, there are serious issues in character. These have empowered a framework in peoples' lives which

[1] Frame: to formulate a concept, play or system

has allowed deceptive belief systems to grow. The sin nature has been cultured, so there has then been a falling away from the Kingdom world.

Allow the cross to work in our life

I dislike immensely being around spirit freaks that lack character. I am going to be straight with you because we need to get this thing right in our understanding. One of the greatest detriments to the body of Christ is when there is a display of gifting that over-awes people and makes them enamoured with the gifting, but there is a lack of character. When the gifting runs out and the anointing just sits, the person eventually falls over because there is a lack of character as the crucible to hold the anointing. You see this time and time again.

Part of growing character is learning about the cross. When life gets tough, who you are will come out. To understand the development of your character and help recognise where you are at, ask yourself whether you are at peace or in complete chaos when things get tough. Oftentimes we will get involved in ministries and start engaging in a pay grade above what our character and level of maturity has been designed to handle, and also beyond what YHVH has required of us. Everything feels so good because of the anointing. All the good things get around us, then suddenly our inner life begins to feel exposed. That is because the anointing will uncover anything that is hidden.

The Word says, *"Therefore endure hardness, as a good soldier of Jesus Christ"* (2 Timothy 2:3). We think hardness means bearing my cross of my spouse or my kids. But your cross is you working out in the secret place of your life the issues that no man knows about. Those are the issues where you have had to destroy the false yoke on your life and walk your way through them. *"My yoke is easy and my burden is light"* (Matthew 11:30). YHVH will always go to the deepest points in your life with character because He wants a bowl honed out for Himself. *"Woe to you, teachers of the law and Pharisees, you hypocrites! You remove fine layers of film and dust from the outside of a cup or bowl, but you leave the inside full of greed and covetousness and self-indulgence"* (Matthew 23:25 VOICE). The Bible talks about how we have been fashioned to be vessels of honour, and vessels of dishonour: *"But in a great house there are not only vessels of gold and of silver, but also of wood and of earth; and some to honor, and some to dishonor. If a man therefore purge himself from these, he shall be a vessel unto honor, sanctified, and fit for the master's use, and prepared unto every good work"* (2 Timothy 2:20-21). Your life can be fashioned in either one of those ways by the measure of the character you carry inside your life.

Love develops character

"We are not recommending ourselves to you again but are giving you a reason to be proud of us, so that you can answer those who are proud of outward things rather than inward character" (2 Corinthians 5:12 ISV).

In this first chapter I want to nail the issues regarding character, because if you do not have character, actually, you have got nothing. I get emails from thousands of people saying, "Ian, in your teaching you said if I do certain things (steps one, two and three), then I can expect certain results. So, I am doing all this expecting that outcome." But, it will not happen unless you have a crucible and a bowl for those things to be put in. One of the reasons that things do not happen for us is because there are holes inside our vessel and things go right through it. Paul says, *"And though I have the gift of prophecy, and understand all mysteries, and all knowledge; and though I have all faith, so that I could remove mountains, and have not love, I am nothing"* (1 Corinthians 13:2). Love is not an emotion. It is not that nice gushy feeling, when you first fall in love with someone. That is only an emotion of love. That is supposed to develop into a character that overcomes, puts other people first, honours others more than yourself and does not condemn others when they make mistakes. It needs to be a character where there is an outworking inside your life of godliness (1 Corinthians 13:4-7).

Character development never stops. You never arrive. The moment you think you have got it all together, YHVH will come and put you in water and soak your bowl, (as a clay vessel) so it all falls to pieces. He wants to remake you into a different thing than you thought you were. So, when you think you have it all together, you really need to know you do not. Character is vital for the ingredient of your spirit man to have a resting place. This bowl that your character develops is very important in order for the seat of your spirit man to be able to flow in the right way. If you are living in chaos, and you engage out of a vessel that is broken, you will only produce chaos around your life. Our character development empowers us to sit above the chaos because we rule over the territory YHVH has given us and so everything is a reflection of heaven on the earth.

People can become hyper-spiritual without understanding that it must be walked out in our life down here where the reflection of who you are in heaven engages in who you are here on earth. It is witnessed by that reflection sitting in the middle of it. The vessel of your character is where your spirit man can sit so what goes on inside that vessel can then be a blessing to multitudes of people around you.

My challenge to you is that you allow YHVH to develop your character. We all know areas in our life where our character needs development. Allow YHVH to do it. I have purposely gone before the Lord and said, "Father, I ask You to break me. Where this is not seated right in my life, break me." You have to be careful of what you ask for. You need to be prepared to walk through things if you do that. But when you walk through things as an overcomer, you will enjoy the fruit of your labour down the line and then you will have fruit in your bowl. These things are essential foundations for spirituality. In this chapter, I am going back to teaching the very beginnings of things that YHVH did with me, because people see all my spirit things, but they fail to see the labour that went in to make it and give it a place to rest properly. It must have a secure seat.

Affirmation must come from YHVH, not spiritual experiences

Character does not develop through you having nice spiritual experiences. In fact, having nice spiritual experiences without the character and the framework for those experiences to sit in disqualifies you. You might want spiritual experiences, but your nature cannot yet contain what YHVH wants to put in it when character has not been developed sufficiently. I think I have had my fair share of spiritual experiences. But when a person gets their fulfillment out of spiritual experiences instead of out of relationship with YHVH, they have a major problem.

If affirmation comes from spiritual experiences, and not out of the relationship with the person of YHVH speaking to you about how much He values you, and who you are intrinsically in Him, then you have a problem. There is nothing wrong with receiving positive affirmation from people. If you cannot receive affirmation from man, then that means that the Father has not affirmed you. If you cannot receive it from man, you will never receive it from the Father. Actually, it is false pride. When people affirm you, you need to learn how to receive what they have to say about you.

Part of the process of character development is being able to receive affirmation and then reflect it in the right way. Reflecting it in the right way is not standing in the front with everybody thanking you and clapping while you say, "It's not me. It's just Jesus!" The issue is that you need to receive affirmation as a human being, but not be built up in pride because of it. The last thing I do at night time is to take a bouquet of flowers back to the presence of the Lord as an offering for the goodness of YHVH in the land of the living, for what people have said to me about that goodness. I go and lay it on the sea of glass and trade it for relationship with the Father (see *Heavenly Trading* in *Realms of the Kingdom Volume 2*), because that is where affirmation must come from. Affirmation must be found in our Father, not in ministry, not in somebody having a relationship with you, not in your husband, your wife, or your kids.

Often times you find a person's identity bound up in their

function for YHVH. When you engage somebody like that in conversation you find everything is about what they do for Yeshua. Yeshua made very succinct statements about that: "*Many will say to me in that day, Lord, Lord, have we not prophesied in your name? and in your name have cast out demons? and in your name done many wonderful works? And then will I profess unto them, I never knew you: depart from me, you that work iniquity*" (Matthew 7:22-23). Their affirmation has come from the things they did for Yeshua. It has not come directly from Him.

YHVH applies pressure to return us to the truth

The development of your character is important to YHVH, because of integrity. You will find that YHVH will put pressure on you in every single area to see if you will hold to the truth or whether you will bend. If you start to bend, you need to go down a pay grade and start dealing with your junk until you can stand the weight of responsibility. Many of the things to do with the Kingdom world that YHVH is trying to release into the earth today are about responsibility. It is about the legislative responsibility of a son.

You can recognise when your character is not developed by how much you try and control everything that is around you. You should be able to let everything go, and allow it to be displayed, instead of trying to control and have your dominion over it. We all need to understand the purpose of the rod and the staff. The rod is about the government of YHVH opening and displaying truth. The staff represents the shepherd's crook that rescues you when you mess up. As YHVH develops your character you will make mistakes, but you are supposed to learn from these times. If you do not learn, YHVH will take you back to it again and again until you get it. Eventually, you will learn that YHVH wants you to die to yourself, come out of that and begin to walk (Luke 9:23-24, Galatians 5:24, Romans 8:12-13). Dying to yourself develops your character because it means loving other people beyond your capacity in human form.

As part of that development, you will find that the worst

darts come from the body of Christ, sometimes like using an AK-47 rifle on full automatic. That is where you must learn to endure hardness as a good soldier of the Lord. You need to understand that because of the identity that YHVH wants to bring us into, if your identity is in the church, YHVH will take you out of that particular part of the church or He will allow us to get hurt by them. We will go through a process to rid us of reliance on the affirmation of people until we find it in our Father. Once we find it in our Father, then everything else will change around us. That is how YHVH develops us.

In the process of walking that process out around us, we need to recognise that our wife or our husband will also develop our character. They will come beside us and say things. If we have any religious junk inside our life, our response will be, "Get behind me! Submit to me," because the real issue is that we have not died. We want others to submit to us to make us feel better in those areas in which we have not yet died. Character is important in family life. Your children will also challenge every black mark in you, because you will grow in them what is in your life, both good and bad. When a child reaches about twelve or thirteen, they will start accusing you because they look at you and recognise their own struggles. Your children can accuse you because it sits in your life. We often respond to them, to do as we say, not as we do. Well, I am sorry, but your children will very likely do what you do, not what you say.

Part of your character development is to understand you must lead the way in dying to yourself. Dying to self and building your character is acknowledging truth (Luke 9:23-24, Galatians 5:24, Romans 8:12-13). When you walk in the truth, you will see the truth and know the truth, and the truth will set you free (John 8:32). We restrict ourselves, so often, by not engaging and acknowledging truth. My kids would come to me and correct me, and often I would say, "Honey, you are right. Today I want to ask your forgiveness. I repent." And they would say, "That's okay, Dad." After that, wow, I would feel so much better.

Character is developed in close relationship with people.

But 'close relationship' does not mean an apostolic network – that is a ministry. True relational connection should be based upon me knowing you and you knowing me, and together sharpening one another. If I see things wrong in you, I can tell you and if you see things wrong in me, you can tell me, because we are building character for integrity's sake, in order to stand in truth in the body of Christ.

YHVH wants us to stand like a pillar in the storm

I want to come back to the crucible. The development of the crucible of who you are as a being is the most important thing that YHVH will look at inside your life. He will engage you to develop this crucible so that who you are and what you are connected with will not fall when pressure comes on it. YHVH wants us to be able to stand in the storm. He wants us to be able to stand in the middle of the storm, to come to the eye of the storm, to find peace in the middle of chaos that seems to swirl around you. YHVH desires to develop your character so that next time the storm comes along you walk right through it, it does not walk right through you. There is a major difference between your reaction to the storms when your character is developed and your reaction to the storms when your character is undeveloped. If your character is undeveloped, you will get angry, bitter, resentful, and frustrated: "*Aahhh!* I kill you!" You know how it goes. Part of the process of life is YHVH bringing us to a point where we can begin to glorify Him in the midst of every sorrow and every triumph.

When you understand the realm of heaven, this world has no effect on you. You live in it, but you are not of it. You do not engage things in it, you engage what is in the Father. And YHVH will develop you to a point where you can walk through the storms of life, and you will not be shaken. You will be like a pillar standing strong through life. Then your job is to train others in how to become a pillar in the same way. The Word says, "*He that overcomes will I make a pillar in the temple of my God, and he shall go no more out: and I will write upon him the name of my God, and the name of the city of my God, which is new Jerusalem, which comes down out of heaven from my God: and I will write upon him my new name"* (Revelation 3:12). By the way, if you do not have those three names, you are not going anywhere.

With everything in the spirit world that is starting to occur today it makes this issue of character is particularly important for the body of Christ. People's identity is woven up in being spiritual. Forget that. Your identity should be woven up in who you are in the Father and your relational connection with Him, which needs to be outworked in your relational connection with those people around you. You need to be in close relationship with them, those who can have input into your life. I have people around me who I have allowed to have input into my life because I need accountability. But this should not be every Tom, Dick and Harry who thinks they have a right to my life. It must be people I am in relationship with. *"Iron sharpens iron; so a man sharpens the countenance of his friend"* (Proverbs 27:17). That word 'friend' means someone who you are in close relationship with, who can see all your flaws, still love you, and yet address the flaws. That, to me, is wonderful; not nice, but wonderful. This develops your character to where you actually can see the love of YHVH. The love of YHVH constrains us. Love commands a response. *"For the love of Christ constrains us; because we thus judge, that if one died for all, then were all dead… they who live should no longer live unto themselves, but unto him who died for them, and rose again."* (2 Corinthians 5:14-15). If your character is not developed, this will create chaos around you, because you try and respond out of the wrong way to protect yourself. Self-protection is another way to recognise undeveloped character.

Allow YHVH to vindicate us

I had one particular circumstance in my life where I was treated unfairly. It affected those I love and the unrefined part of me wanted to get an AK-47 rifle. Over that time the Lord came to me and said, "Son, I want you to get up your mountain. Stay and pray. Do not give them a man to fight with. Shut your mouth!" *"You will not have to fight this battle. Take up your positions; stand firm and see the deliverance the Lord will give you…"*

(2 Chronicles 20:17). That was one of the hardest things to do, especially when I saw what it was doing to my family. I am sharing this to show you that even though you and I have experienced many things, YHVH will still come in and engage us to see what we are going to do in certain situations. Three years later that other ministry did not exist anymore. Then, the test of character was whether I would rejoice over someone else's failure, or bless and release them. YHVH justified me, and in that process I have learned that allowing YHVH to vindicate us is very important. It develops our character in a major way. Will we rejoice over an enemy when he falls, or will we bless him in his falling and bless him on his way? Character is displayed in our ability to refrain our hand when we think we have a right to act, to hold our hand away. Even though difficulties exist around us, we can put a framework around them without having to kick them about.

When you start to deal with things in the spirit and your character is a mess, the first thing that will be displayed in your life is your brokenness. The enemy will come after that because he knows the crucible of your character has not been developed well enough yet. Pride is usually connected with spirituality. Where we have pride, our character lacks the foundation of having walked through our issues in Christ. Somewhere along in our line, we are stuck. It is essential to engage with YHVH to allow Him access in a personal way. By the way, allowing YHVH access does not mean going to somebody for twenty-five years of counseling. That seems to happen today because people can become addicted to the counselor.

Spiritual experiences do not guarantee maturity

Please do not make the mistake of believing because you see and have spiritual experiences, that you are mature in YHVH. It simply means you are having spiritual experiences. It does not mean you are a mature person either. People come to me, and assume they are mature because they have all these spiritual experiences. Having a spiritual experience does not mean much at all. Do not go after spiritual experiences instead of going after the development of relationship. It is only relationship which matures character because when you are in relationship with someone, they will call you out on 'who's who' and 'what's what' inside your life. In other words, they will be straight with you. If we cannot handle people being straight with us in this arena it is actually because our character has not been developed enough. So, when somebody gets too direct with us, telling us 'who's who' and 'what's what' about our life, we gallop off into the sunset like the Lone Ranger in the 1950s television series. He is called the Lone Ranger for a reason, because he only has one friend, Tonto, who is always with him, speaking to him and agreeing with him (a bit like a familiar spirit). Lone rangers in the body of Christ are those who want to maintain lordship over all their own issues, instead of allowing Christ to speak into them. Christ is not your Tonto, by the way.

Character affects the vessel or framework that our spiritual experiences are supposed to fit into. If there are flaws in the vessel, then your experiences will also be flawed. It will become all about you: what your abilities are, who you are, who you think you are, and what you want other people to think you are. You then present an image of something that is totally incorrect, without the true character to handle the responsibility. Spiritual experiences must lead to spiritual responsibility. This does not mean engaging in spiritual warfare. We are supposed to live in the realm of the government of YHVH where there is no spiritual warfare. The only warfare is about our position. That is what all spiritual warfare is about. It is not about wrestling against a demon. It is a wrestling for our position over a demon. Sometimes the church has wrongly taught us to look *up* to something. I have taught on some of this; (see Realms of the Kingdom Volume 2 Trading in the heavens, *Dealing with Spiritual Attack* and my MP3 series: *Kingdom Government Teaching Set). YHVH* I discuss the court system, how it functions, and some of the processes and protocols related to that.

Turning our back on the line in the sand

The way YHVH frames our character is through the fiery trials of life where we must make little incremental choices in the right direction. We think the choices we make can be decided based upon an imaginary line in the sand. We try and categorise sin: that side is sin, and this side is holy. Well, actually, by your incremental choices you can put your little toe over into sin. Then the line has to move just a little bit more. The line must move because now you think it is okay to do that certain thing. That is the thing about a line: it will always extend out in front of you, and will not be a boundary any longer. That is because the natural human tendency is to put our toe over the line. It is a complete life's direction through the little incremental changes every day.

Character makes a decision to turn your back altogether on the line in the sand. Now, you do not even look at the line, or at what you think is sin, and what is not sin. You do not look at what the boundaries are. When you turn your back on something, you must look at a different source other than the line in the sand. Whatever you look at is what you are going to become. So you must set your eyes in the right place to enable YHVH to begin to engage you in the right way. We want to live half our life with one foot over that side of the line, and one foot over the other side of the line. We look this way with the hope that we can look that way occasionally. That is the way most humans live unless, like Noah, your DNA is pure and you are perfect in your genetics (Genesis 6:9). See Realms of the Kingdom Volume 1, the chapter *The DNA of YHVH*. Actually, the line in the sand indicates your need to turn your back on it, because repentance to a Hebrew is completely different from the interpretation given to us by Greek thinking. Repentance to a Hebrew is turning back towards the face of YHVH in awe, and coming back into the revelation of the awe of YHVH again. It is not saying, "I'm sorry, I'm sorry," and then still putting our foot over that side of the line again. Then turning this way and repeating, "I'm sorry, I'm sorry." These are character keys that have rarely been taught in church life but are important in our life going forward.

When YHVH starts to engage us, and we turn in awe with our eyes in the right place, we learn to understand a different government. The word 'understand' in the heavenly court setting means "I submit my life to your authority". We must turn away from the line, towards the Father, and lift our eyes to the hill, to the right place, to the right mountain. *"I will lift up my eyes unto the hills, from which comes my help"* (Psalm 121:1). When we understand that mountain, it has jurisdiction over our life. When we continually look at the line in the sand, then it has jurisdiction over our life. Character involves making continual choices to turn to the right Source, for the right supply.

Spiritual experiences should come out of relationship with YHVH

As I have said, simply engaging spiritual experiences and pursuing them is the wrong thing to do. Spiritual experiences are supposed to come out of relationship with YHVH, wanting to know Him, who He is, what He is, what He does, watching Him when He does things, being there when He does things, and learning how to do them. When we do it wrong, we get disciplined and we learn how to do it right (Hebrews 12:5-11). These encounters are supposed to bring maturity so we can handle responsibility and spiritual experiences.

People say to me, "Oh, I've been doing this and that in heaven. I went and slayed this and I did that." But only when I see you in some of the governmental arenas in heaven do I know you have been given delegated responsibility. Everything that I teach is not simply about what you 'do' in heaven. It is actually about the responsibility YHVH has given you to function in the Father's house, in that world, ground out into this world down here. And the grounding out down here is all about character. Because let me tell you, if there are issues inside you that the enemy has got his finger on, then your spiritual experiences will eventually get mixed up in those little things that are inside your life. This journey is not about getting 'goose-bumps on your goose-bumps' with spiritual experiences. Actually, they should be called *'pig-bumps'*, because a pig is all about himself: how much he can get, when he wants it and as much as he wants. Spiritual experiences often only drive us into wanting more of them, not wanting a deeper relationship with Him.

YHVH disciplines us because He loves us

I love the way YHVH has framed human beings and made us in His image. We each need revelation of what that image was before the fall. Then we would understand the love YHVH has for us. One of the highest spiritual experiences we can have is to know who we were in Him before sin entered into the world and who we are now, free from sin (Romans 6:18). Then, the love of YHVH will become a foundation for discipline in our life. YHVH does not discipline us out of irritation, He disciplines us because He so abundantly loves us (Hebrews 12:6). The Word tells us that we must not despise His discipline (Proverbs 3:11, Hebrews 12:5), and yet most of us do not want it. Those chastisements come from people sitting right next to you, your spouse, your close family and friends. But often times, we cannot recognise they are from Him because we are not looking into the face of YHVH, and we are not seeing Him.

Our heart is connected to YHVH's love

People ask: "How can I see YHVH?" The Bible says, *"Blessed are the pure in heart: for they shall see YHVH"* (Matthew 5:8). You get pure in heart by what your heart meditates on and thinks about. Out of the issues of your heart the mouth speaks, and out of the abundance of the heart your life flows. *"A good man out of the good treasure of his heart brings forth that which is good... for of the abundance of the heart his mouth speaks"* (Luke 6:45). *"Keep your heart with all diligence; for out of it are the issues of life"* (Proverbs 4:23). Everything comes out of your heart. The heart is about the four rivers of YHVH that are supposed to flow out of your belly (John 7:38), watering the earth that is around us, bringing life into all the earth[2]. YHVH wants to bring life, and it is all about your heart.

[2] For more teaching on this subject see *The Garden of Your Heart* chapter in Realms of the Kingdom Volume 2

Your heart is connected to love. *"Though I speak with the tongues of men and of angels, and have not love, I am become as sounding brass, or a clanging cymbal"* (1 Corinthians 13:1). YHVH wants to engage us inside our heart in love. When we do engage in love, YHVH is then free in His ownership of us because: *"Love suffers long and is kind; love does not envy; love does not parade itself, is not puffed up; does not behave rudely, does not seek its own, is not provoked, thinks no evil; does not rejoice in iniquity, but rejoices in the truth; bears all things, believes all things, hopes all things, endures all things. Love never fails"* (1 Corinthians 13:4-8 NKJV). Reading through 1 John 1, 2, and 3, and looking at the book of John itself to see what Yeshua did will help you understand what love is.

Yeshua chose to emotionally connect with only twelve people, yet the church often expects their pastor to connect with all the people in the church. Yeshua had three that He was more closely connected to (Peter, James and John), and of those three, just one, John, with whom He was deeply acquainted. John has authority to speak about love because of this relationship. YHVH is omniscient (all-knowing – Isaiah 40:13-14, John 3:20) and omnipresent (present everywhere – Jeremiah 23:23-24, Psalm 139:7-10). He can do more than we can, yet in His fleshly form, He did not relate intimately with everyone. He did bring correction to everything that was around Him. Wherever Yeshua went, He said, "I really love you... *smack, smack*! I really care for you but if you keep doing this... *smack, smack!"(Mark 8:33)*. He did not say, "Oh, *Lovey-Dovey*, you are so nice. I so love you" That is because love is not an emotion. It is a choice, an act of your will. Choosing to love means sometimes it is going to be tough, not easy. The rubber meets the road in your character when it gets really tough on the inside. You have to grind out the corn of your life into powder so YHVH can begin to use it for His own Kingdom. Yes, it is hard, but character is what forms the essential crucible.

How YHVH framed '*Adam*'

We have no true idea of YHVH's desire when He framed and formed '*Adam*' (man). Even Hebraically, we do not properly understand how YHVH made humankind. To a Hebrew, YHVH is breath *"The spirit of God has made me, and the breath of the Almighty has given me life"* (Job 33:4). YHVH created 'Adam' out of the glory of the river Pishon which carried pure gold dust from heaven onto the earth, *"The first, the Pishon, flows around the land of Havilah – a rich land plentiful in gold of premium quality, bdellium, and onyx stones"* (Genesis 2:11-12 VOICE). He did not create 'Adam' out of dirt. There were no plants at that time to decompose. Gold dust was the only dust on the earth in those days. So, YHVH formed 'Adam' out of this super-conductor of light (gold). He then took Himself, who is Breath, and put Himself into 'Adam' (Genesis 2:7). 'Adam' inhaled, breathing in YHVH. When 'Adam' breathed out YHVH came out, and YHVH was looking at a complete reflection of Himself, the first God-like man (Genesis 1:26-27). That is the reason Yeshua breathed on His disciples (John 20:22). He did the same thing. He returned them to their first estate. That is why they could go two-by-two bringing signs and wonders. When they came back they said, *"Lord, even the demons are subject unto us through your name"* (Luke 10:17). But Yeshua replied, *"Nevertheless in this rejoice not, that the spirits are subject unto you; but rather rejoice, because your names are written in heaven"* (Luke 10:20). Yeshua admonished them not to look at the signs and wonders, because that should be a normal part of our breath enabled by the *yechida*[3] within us. The *yechida* is the flame or the God-spark inside a person. It is this life-spark within that empowers a person to sacrifice or even give their life for the sake of their love of YHVH.

To put a framework around something, you must first understand the fullness of the life that was there before the framework. So, for YHVH to frame *Adam* He had full understanding of the life that was there. YHVH called him *'Adam'* which in Hebrew means "a doorway to the government

[3] Strongs Concordance from the root word: 3173. Yachid: feminine הָדִיחְי as substantive Psalm 22:21; Psalm 35:17 יִתָדִיחְי my *only one*, poetic for *my life*, as the one unique and priceless possession which can never be replaced (in each יִשְׁפַנ).

of a never-ending supply of the River of YHVH (we will unpack this understanding in a later chapter)." In the fullness of what He put into *Adam*, YHVH put into the world a never-ending supply of His own life, coming through a person. YHVH frames things into existence with His voice, exhaling. Everything framed is supposed to be on the breath because that is the way YHVH first framed everything. *"And YHVH said, Let there be light: and there was light."* (Genesis 1:3); *"And YHVH said, Let there be a firmament in the midst of the waters, and let it divide the waters from the waters"* (V6). He framed *Adam* by breathing into him because YHVH is breath.

Everything flows on the breath. YHVH wants to unlock the framework, but to understand the framework you need to understand the truth of what was there first. He wants us to get the revelation in our character about the truth of who we really are in Him first, before we have all the spiritual experiences. Once we have this revelation, the spiritual experiences fit in their right place. Then we will chase intimacy instead of spiritual experiences. Intimacy involves returning back to the awe and wonderment of YHVH. It is a conscious choice we have to make each day, to turn towards that, so YHVH can come into us in the fullness of what we were created to be. That is why He called us *'Adam'*.

I love the way the law of the firstborn operates in our favour to bring grace and mercy into our lives. The firstborn receives judgement, the second born receives grace and mercy. So the person who was the firstborn son of a family would take responsibility for the complete family. Adam was the first-born, we are the second-born because we are in Christ. Christ is called the Last Adam (1 Corinthians 15:45) so that on the first Adam there could be judgement while on the second Adam there is grace. Then Jesus became the first-born son who received judgement, so that as second-born sons, we could receive grace (Colossians 1:15,18). We live under a dispensation of grace because grace empowers us to turn the right way (Titus 2:11-12). The law of the firstborn comes into play when you go into a safe city, and heaven is a safe haven for us. When we go into heaven, the charges that have come against us have to be levied against Yeshua because there He is the firstborn. When we run into Him, He becomes our rescuer. The charges against us go after Him. He has already paid the price, so we get grace and mercy given out to us.

YHVH has caused us to live under a dispensation of grace so that grace will empower us to turn the right way. Grace is not some emotional thing: it is actually the power and the will to do YHVH's will. That is what grace really is. It is a conscious choice to embrace the desire of YHVH for your life out of your awe and wonder of YHVH. Grace is the empowerment and will to turn towards Him, so that we can build a framework for Him to sit in. (Philippians 2:13) That framework is only built out of relationship with Him, the other side of the veil, by faith. The framework for YHVH to sit in is not built out of having spiritual experiences. I constantly meet people around the world saying, "Oh I am doing this, and I am chasing that..." But my interest is not in your spiritual experiences. I want to know about your character. What does your spouse say about your life, what do your kids say, how do your family or other people you relate with experience your attitudes and choices?

The deception of social media

In some ways I despise the internet and social media like Facebook, because people are not looking at your real life when you are on Facebook. You can pretend to be something you are not. No one knows because they do not see your home life or what you are like when no one is looking. You can put up a facade, a deceptive image. That is why it is so important to personally connect with people in real life. They will put their finger on the things wrong inside your life and say, "Oh, I don't think so!" But we do not enjoy that, so we use Facebook to avoid relating intimately. There are now "internet churches" around the world. You sit in front of your screen watching live streaming. That is your 'church'. You tithe to them, but you do not have to really relate to anyone.

Actually, it is all about deception. The Church of Antioch

looked a lot different. Part of the fallenness of man is the deception associated with lack of relationship, and lack of personal connection one with another. This is so important. If you do not allow YHVH's dealings inside your life, you will find that you will have spiritual experiences but eventually they will lead to deception because your character is not developed sufficiently so it cannot hold what YHVH is doing around your life. If you love YHVH, He will love you enough to bring you where you need to be, and to have all you need. Out of my relationship with YHVH, I have had all these weird and wonderful things happen, but I have never gone after them. I have only ever pursued knowing Him intimately, knowing how to do what He is doing, watching Him do it. I want to see and understand all that process.

I have walked with a guy named Karl for six or seven years now. I originally had a discipleship-mentorship relationship with him, which after about three years developed into a friendship. It was not until about two years ago that I made the decision to open my heart to become a friend with him. That meant I had to change, to let go of being instructor and teacher, and to actually build a relationship.

With my children, we have gone through the stages of teaching and training. But then, I made a conscious choice to become friends with my kids.

It is only out of friendship that a deeper relationship can form and life can be ground out in this arena because, relationally, you are now discipling people to take your place.

Yeshua personally discipled only twelve people to take His place. If Yeshua only dealt with twelve, do not try to do it with five thousand. Do not seek to become the centre of something in which you cannot personally disciple and see each person's life. Understanding these things is vital for where we are going in the future, and for what YHVH wants to do inside the earth.

Love is the barometre of your spiritual life

Remember, I said love is not a feeling. Love is an act of your will, which means you must make right choices. We often struggle to choose correctly either because we like what we have, or we do not know how to get something else. It is never that we cannot. The process with love comes down to realising that if we love YHVH, then we need to learn to relate with Him in a completely different way. We need to learn how to fulfill His life rather than having Him fulfill ours. That means we must put Him first. Love does not want its own (1 Corinthians 13:5). So we must put Him first. Putting Him first is hard work, but character is displayed by putting other people first. "Love does not want its own" means I do not want my own way, and I want what is best for you. My job is to make you the most successful you can be at any given time, to help you become what you need to be. Relationship with your husband or wife should be exactly the same way: "I love you so much I want to see you become the best you can be." We have to grind those things out. Those who have been married over thirty years know it is not easy. You have to walk through this. After thirty years of marriage you are just starting to mature. You are beginning to understand that it is not about feelings, it is a choice.

Love is the barometre of your spiritual life. Spiritual experiences are not a barometre of your spiritual life. The barometre of your spiritual life is about love, because love builds character inside you. Love destroys your sin nature by putting other people first. Love then becomes a grounding force that gives us the ability to walk into YHVH when we do not want to. It gives us the ability to find life when we are in death, and to find joy when there is heartache. Love unlocks YHVH's ability within us.

Our supply is the other side of the veil

The supply of what you need is only found the other side of the veil. You cannot walk out your life with YHVH this side of the veil. In later chapters I will discuss being a priest, what it really means to be a priest, and how to go through the veil. We need to understand that process. So often in our church life we try to pull heaven's supply down here: "Father we pull this down." "Lord, fill the atmosphere with Your presence." Well, who has moved? The Bible says He is omnipresent (Jeremiah 23:23-24, Psalm 139:7-10), which means He is already here, so the issue is you going into that Presence, not it coming before you. These are major misunderstandings. We try to pull everything down towards us, but we are meant to go in towards it, into the middle of that supply, to engage all of that, and then *bring* it to this side, because holiness is a choice. Holiness is another part of character. But you cannot become holy without righteousness, and righteousness is a gift we receive the other side of the veil. We often try to become holy by making right choices outside of the gift of righteousness. We often try to discipline our life so that we do not do wrong anymore. But YHVH is not interested in a disciplined life. He is interested in a dead life. A dead life is only found the other side of the veil, where you are given righteousness. So, we need to go in and engage righteousness. Then, out of the supply of righteousness, we can bring righteousness back here, which will empower holiness (Ephesians 4:24, 1 Corinthians 1:30).

Love empowers holiness because love is the right choice

True repentance is making right choices to turn your back on the line and to be set apart, which is holiness. Continually saying, "I am sorry. I put my toe over the line" is Christian schizophrenia. Paul was schizophrenic: *"For that which I do I know not: for what I would, that do I not; but what I hate, that do I… For the good that I would I do not: but the evil which I would not, that I do. Now if I do that which I would not, it is no more I that do it, but sin that dwells in me"* (Romans 7:15,19 -20). So, even Paul understood Christian schizophrenia. He also understood freedom in Christ through the veil. *"I thank YHVH through Jesus Christ our Lord… There is therefore now no condemnation to them who are in Christ Jesus, who walk not after the flesh, but after the Spirit. For the law of the Spirit of life in Christ Jesus has made me free from the law of sin and death"* (Romans 7:25-8:2). So the issue is actually turning your back on the line in the sand and being in Christ, in His world where he is. The act of repentance means turning back towards the perfect state of awe and the wonderment of who YHVH is. It means keeping your eyes hooked into that right place, through the veil. Love empowers holiness because love is the right choice: you must learn to love YHVH first, then yourself, then others as yourself as scripture says. In that empowerment YHVH then begins to release to us.

Character is not developed alone or in your prayer closet. It is developed in relationship with others on earth, and also in relationship with the saints of old that have gone before us. These are the men in white linen[4] that are around us and who make a way. Actually, they will beat you about as much as the people here as you start walking with them in the glory realms. They want the reward more than you do, so they will discipline you until you do what you are supposed to *"Therefore seeing we also are surrounded with so great a cloud of witnesses, let us lay aside every weight, and the sin which does so easily ensnare us, and let us run with patience the race that is set before us"* (Hebrews 12:1). That is why you have relationship, one with another. That is why John says, *"Beloved, let us love one another: for love is of YHVH; and everyone that loves is born of YHVH, and knows YHVH"* (1 John 4:7). *"Look not every man on his own things, but every man also on the things of others"* (Philippians 2:4). So, again, the issue is love. And people in relationship around you will discipline you because this is where it gets ground out, in relationship down here. Character grinds all these wrong things out down here. That is why it is crucial. Of all the chapters in this book, this is the one I want you to read over and over. It is the most important one.

We must walk through this, and it is only walked out in personal relationship, one with another, especially when it gets tough. That is when it really gets ground out. I would not swap what I have gone through, where YHVH gave me a dream and it has not come to pass. I had to wrestle with my own internal issues, and still come out on the top, realising that YHVH does not change (Malachi 3:6). Only the process of what He is doing and how He is going to do it changes. Those experiences build character in us like nothing else does.

There are other situations I can remember, difficult situations

[4] See the Men in White Linen chapter in Realms of the Kingdom Volume 2

in my life and times I was unjustly treated. Years later, looking back I was so glad I had walked through it. Everything is about character. I want you to see those trials were not about 'goose-bumps on my goose-bumps'. They were ground out in this life, where we learn how to overcome. It is only overcoming in this life that warrants our position in that life (1 John 5:4-5). There is no other way to do it, and YHVH will take us through it.

Activation

Father, we want to thank You that we can come into Your presence. We do that now, just attentively turning our eyes towards You, Yeshua.

Lord we honour You for Your abandoned love for us, that while we were yet sinners You died for us. Father, I ask that You would begin to engage the readers in this arena of character development in their lives. Father I ask that you would hold us, that You would not stop pushing at us, You would not stop working with us until the coming of your Son's manifestation in us.

Father, I ask for those who read these words, that You would quicken all of this to them, quicken this message to their hearts. Father, we ask that we would begin to walk into the fullness of You, like Yeshua, who had to develop His character for thirty years, and then it was refined in three and a half years. Father, I want to thank You for Your love. Lord, I honor Your presence. We honor You today, Father. We thank You that even though we have messed it up, You have not let us go. You have made a conscious choice, Father, because Your Word says that You are love. You made that choice, Father, that while we were messed up, You would not let go and You never will let go. Father, thank You. In the name of Yeshua. Amen.

CHAPTER 2
THE LAW OF FAITH

There are many laws that the Bible mentions that we do not understand or we do not understand their application to our lives. We also fail to understand their appropriation for who we are today and what we are able to do because the law is in place. We need to understand these laws and what they can input into our lives. If you function by those laws, you will find that everything around you will move to bless you within those laws because those laws are good things to have around you. For example, the Law of Faith is an amazing thing. If you understood the Law of Faith you could just stand and operate under that Law of Faith and everything around you would move.

The Law of Faith is one of the key laws that we need to begin to submit our lives to. It is the realm of the Kingdom that is associated with faith. Paul makes this amazing statement "*… The life which I now live in the flesh I live by the faith of the Son of God, who loved me, and gave himself for me*" (Galatians 2:20).

This is the Establishment of the Law of Faith. Paul recognised that, even though he had faith in everything, it still would not be enough. He had to shift the law of the belief in himself and the capacity that YHVH gave him to facilitate things here to what Jesus did and operate out of Yeshua's faith.

The life I now live I live by the faith of the Son of YHVH. Here you have Jesus in the realm of the Kingdom, now with a full understanding and a fuller ability to appropriate everything out of that arena of the Kingdom on and around your life.

So instead of you supplying what is needed and you working your way through stuff, you actually engage His faith. Turn from your own supply and self sufficiency into His faith and entangle yourself around it saying, "Lord, that faith that is there, I draw on that because that is how I live my life. It is by Your faith, not trusting in my own faith."

You can build your own faith. The Bible tells us that we need to have faith. *"But without faith it is impossible to please him: for he that comes to God must believe that he is, and that he is a rewarder of them that diligently seek him"* (Hebrews 11:6).

There is a lower level of faith which is about your faith, about what you can do and your abilities to do it: You need faith to exercise and operate the mandate for whatever you are called to do. You need to have faith when you lay hands on someone that they will be healed or delivered. You need to have faith in your own life that the demon is going to go. You even need to have faith when you are counselling someone that YHVH is going to speak through you.

This is your own faith. It is a lower form of faith. There is a higher form of faith which is the faith of the Son of God. He has already done everything, and accomplished it all. What I have to do now is to shift it from me and the arenas I have walked in, to bring myself under the government of Yeshua's faith.

When that begins to happen, everything starts changing because suddenly it is no longer coming out of me, it is coming upon me.

YHVH wants us to live with the King's faith. The Bible says of Jesus that, "...The government shall be upon his shoulder" (Isaiah 9:6). "...As you, Father, are in me, and I in you, that they also may be one in us" (John 17:21). If I am in Christ, and Christ is in the Father, and I am one with Yeshua, and He is one with the Father, it means that the government is going to rest on my shoulders. The law unleashes the government of heaven to manifest around your life.

You see it is all about what the laws do. They put us into a functional arena where we have the capacity to download and bring something that normally was not there, and to orchestrate and administrate things out of the realm of the Kingdom. The laws are vitally important for us. Many of us have seen the laws as a hindrance and a boundary and we have wrestled to try and get out of the laws. There is one law that you have got to get out of and that is the 'law of sin and death'. That is the law you have got to get out of, but you have got to get into the others. The only way you can get out of the law of sin and death is to get into the life-giving laws *"For the law of the Spirit of life in Christ Jesus has made me free from the law of sin and death"* (Romans 8:2).

It is not good enough to just take the law of sin and death away. You have got to go into Christ who is the author of the law of the Spirit of life. Everything in the Kingdom is about going somewhere – going from one place to another, from one line to another line, from glory to glory, line upon line, precept upon precept. YHVH wants us to reveal these things in the world around us. Usually the laws that YHVH puts in place are immovable. They bring a divine expression of His government through your life and into the earth that is around you. The church needs to come into the governmental arena of the Kingdom because, once we are in that governmental arena, you can do anything in the realm of the spirit. The government that is behind the laws that you submit to will actually stand behind you. You can go declare to the mountain to move and it will move. It will just move because you are moving. It will stand because you are standing and when you say go it will go. When you say come here it will come here.

Jesus said to His disciples "If you have faith as a grain of mustard seed, you shall say unto this mountain, Remove from here to yonder place; and it shall remove; and nothing shall be impossible unto you. (Matt 17:20 King James 2000 Bible).

You need to step into the law of faith, become part of it and submit your life to it. It then unleashes the whole arena of the Kingdom's power, its mandate and authority to operate in this area, because everything that you have ever thought possible for your life comes out of that arena. *"...Whosoever shall say unto this mountain, Be removed, and be cast into the sea; and shall not doubt in his heart, but shall believe that those things which he said shall come to pass; he shall have whatsoever he said"* (Mark 11:23).

"And Jesus answering said unto them, Have faith in God" (Mark 11:22. This is the Lord saying, "Have faith in Me because, when you have faith in me, I have a law that functions higher than the law that you live by and, when you have faith in Me, you will see it happen". We struggle so much because we have been taught that it is all about us and what we have to do in this arena here. Actually, it has nothing to do with us. That is the lower law. It is about the operation of the Kingdom of God on the earth, and what you do in the Kingdom of God on the earth.

So what YHVH is looking for is the government that unleashes His faith around your life. You can respond by saying "Lord, I have faith in what You have done for me, and what You are going to do. Lord, I draw on Your faith today. All that I need out of that arena for this to facilitate, I draw on it and stand in it and I stand under it so that Your government can rest upon this thing". When faith from Him comes upon it, everything begins to change.

In Acts 15:9 Paul talks about being sanctified by faith. *"And God, who knows the hearts, bore them witness, giving them the Holy Spirit, even as he did unto us; And put no difference between us and them, purifying their hearts by faith"* (Acts 15:8-9).

Paul knew about the law of faith. The law of faith sanctifies us and makes us holy. When you are trusting in someone who has already done it, you are drawing on the supply of all that He has already done. Because He is holy and righteous, you become holy and righteous. There are no works involved. You just submit to it and it just happens. It is like stepping into the Kingdom. You do not get clean to go, you go to get clean.

This is how some of these laws operate. You function underneath them and they make things happen . There is then nothing anyone can do. It is just what is going to happen.

YHVH honours and empowers what He has already done. So when you submit your life to Him, with the whole arena of the government of the law of faith, He honours and empowers that thing around your life.

What is the faith of the Son of YHVH? It is bigger than anything in me or around me. The Law of the faith of the Son of YHVH has the final say. It speaks of His death, the power of His blood, and the authority and promise of His resurrection. Having faith in the Son of YHVH means that I believe that whatever YHVH will do, He will do for me. It is not dependent on me.

"And when the disciples saw Him walking on the sea, they were troubled, saying, "It is a ghost!" And they cried out for fear. But immediately Jesus spoke to them, saying, "Be of good cheer! It is I; do not be afraid." And Peter answered Him and said, "Lord, if it is You, command me to come to You on the water." So He said, "Come." And when Peter had come down out of the boat, he walked on the water to go to Jesus. ***30*** *But when he saw that the wind was boisterous, he was afraid; and beginning to sink he cried out, saying, "Lord, save me!" And immediately Jesus stretched out His hand and caught him, and said to him, "O you of little faith, why did you doubt?" And when they got into the boat, the wind ceased* (Matthew 14:26-32 NKJV).

This is a great scripture that illustrates the ability to lock into the law of faith. Peter did not step out of the boat and walk on the water out of his own faith. Jesus spoke a word to him. "Come". The moment Jesus said, "Come", the law of faith came into operation. On that understanding of the law of faith, Peter plugged into the word "Come". He started to walk on the water, plugged into that word. The Word then says he started to look around him and then he began to notice the wind and waves. What happened was, he shifted from the law of faith into his own faith which started to make him sink into the water. You cannot walk on water out of your own faith. It must operate out of the law of faith

Stretching out, Peter took hold of the law of faith. Jesus was already walking on the water. The Bible says He picked him up. Operating out of the law of faith is about putting your hand into the source of the supply of the law. That .then gives a foundation for you to step into the things of the Kingdom.

Historically, it has been taught that it was Peter's faith to walk on the water. I do not see it like that. I see that it was the law of faith operating. When Peter moved into his own faith, he started sinking. Peter cried out to the Lord, so Jesus stretched out His hand again, picked him up and went back to the boat. The Bible continues "O you of little faith, why did you doubt?" It is not talking about doubting his own faith. It is talking about doubting Jesus' faith. This is a good example of the law of faith operating that released the power of the law of faith.

"Then said Martha unto Jesus, Lord, if you had been here, my brother would not have died. But I know, that even now, whatsoever you will ask of God, God will give it to you. Jesus said unto her, Your brother shall rise again" (John 11:21-23).

Martha had tapped into the law of faith knowing that whatever Jesus said was going to come to pass. Living it out of His faith and not her own. Then Jesus went to the tomb and raised Lazarus from the dead, *"Jesus said unto her, Said I not unto you, that, if you would believe, you should see the glory of God? Then they took away the stone from the place where the dead was laid. And Jesus lifted up his eyes, and said, Father, I thank you that you have heard me. And I knew that you hear me always: but because of the people who stand by I said it, that they may believe that you have sent me. And when he thus had spoken, he cried with a loud voice, Lazarus, come forth. And he that was dead came forth, bound hand and foot with grave clothes: and his face was bound about with a cloth. Jesus said unto them, Loose him, and let him go"* (John 11:40-44).

There are examples throughout the scriptures of Jesus doing signs and wonders like this. It is teaching us how to plug into the law of faith. Often, one of the greatest things that we struggle with is praying to raise the dead. That requires a higher law than your own faith when you come into that situation (and my prayer is that you will have an opportunity to raise someone from the dead). When you have done it once, you will be able to do it again and again. It will begin to happen more and more quickly. What happens is that it is the law of faith that empowers you to raise someone from the dead. It is not your faith.

The way that we have been taught in church is that you need to have faith to pray to raise the dead. No – you need to have faith in Him, that when you pray to raise a person, His faith and His law are going to start to take precedence over the dead body. And because He is going to empower His own faith, you and I are just going to be the channels for that to travel through our lives.

You need to practice drawing on the law of faith. I used to dream about praying for people who were dead and people who were demonised. After about a year and a half, it started happening. I am now dreaming about raising the dead and walking through walls. I am drawing on the law of faith so that I will raise somebody from the dead. It is not going to be by my faith. I know I do not have faith to raise somebody from the dead. Yet I do have faith for growing legs. Growing legs is easy. It is just going to happen because I have faith for that to happen. It is the same power but when it comes to something that is challenging for me, then I need a higher law operating. When I am submitted to that law and that law functions around my life, it becomes very exciting!

This brings me to a recurring issue concerning faith that disturbs me. When somebody prays for you and you do not get healed, they often say your faith was not strong enough. Or the person who prayed for you may think their own faith was not strong enough to believe for healing to happen. Not getting healed may have nothing to do with your faith or their faith. Healing has to do with Yeshua's faith. We need to understand the operation or the functionality of the Law of Faith. In Galatians 2:20 the Word says; *"I am crucified with Christ: nevertheless I live; yet not I, but Christ lives in me: and the life which I now live in the flesh I live by the faith of the Son of God, who loved me, and gave himself for me."* The Word says that I am to live by faith, not that I simply function by it. So I must be walking in faith. The law of faith is total trust in the provision of another for my life and engaging the other so that this full provision can become mine. By extension, the law of faith is about relationship.

The law of faith enables you to tap into the flow of the presence and Glory of YHVH without any work. At any given time, the law of faith enables us to have instant power, instant authority, instant governmental right and instant healing. It is like putting your fingers into a 400-volt socket.

The law of faith is like that. Once you grab it, it will affect everyone around your life. It releases instant power onto the face of the earth around you. It is the most amazing thing. In Asia there were about 3000- 4000 people in a meeting and I could feel this demonic spirit that was brooding over the meeting. It was in the lives of the people there because it was over their family lines and what they had been given over to. I reached out my hand and said, "Lord, I reach into that law that dictates Your government on the face of the earth. Father I release that now". The moment I did that I had 3000 or more people manifesting on the floor, like snakes, getting deliverance. That was not my faith. All I did was tap into the power source, like putting my finger into the socket, getting hold of it and releasing it.

It is amazing to watch the law of faith operate. I do not have faith for everything yet but I know there is a higher law. And because I have practiced drawing on it, dreaming about it, putting my hand into it and allowing the government to come upon my shoulders, it can be facilitated here. For it to become easy, you need to practice it.

The law of faith is based on the rock of Christ that lives inside of you. Each of us has a boundary stone, a living stone, in us. The Bible calls us living stones (1 Peter 2:5). That Living Stone becomes the foundation for the law of faith to rest upon. The law of faith vibrates with that stone. When they come together, the molecules are, vibrating at the same frequency and in that instant, information gets transferred. When you tap into it, this rock comes alive with the same power that is there and it instantly becomes available inside your life. You have this in you. You have the capacity to tap into the law of faith and, when you do, everything in the realm of the spirit in your life, and those around you, will begin to change. It just begins to happen. It is like electricity that spreads out over a meeting. It is amazing to watch it happen.

Abraham justified by Faith

I remember the powerful encounter I had with Melchizedek the night I first wrote this talk on the Law of Faith. In faith, Abraham foreshadowed the Father giving us His Son, *"By faith Abraham, when he was tested, offered up Isaac: and he that had received the promises offered up his only begotten son. Of whom it was said, That in Isaac shall your descendants be called"* (Hebrews 11:17-18). It was not his own faith but "accounting that God was able to raise him up, even from the dead; from which also he received him in a figure". YHVH looks for a shadow of Himself to rest on and Abraham gave Him that shadow on behalf of us all. But there is so much more in Abraham's faith walk that we might have missed.

Scripture tells us that a great battle took place among several kings of the region, *"...four kings against five. Then they took all the goods of Sodom and Gomorrah, and all their provisions, and went their way. They also took Lot, Abram's brother's son who dwelt in Sodom, and his goods, and departed.*

Then one who had escaped came and told Abram the Hebrew, Now when Abram heard that his brother was taken captive, he armed his three hundred and eighteen trained servants who were born in his own house, and went in pursuit as far as Dan. He divided his forces against them by night, and he and his servants attacked them and pursued them as far as Hobah, which is north of Damascus. So he brought back all the goods, and also brought back his brother Lot and his goods, as well as the women and the people. And the king of Sodom went out to meet him at the Valley of Shaveh (that is, the King's Valley), after his return from the defeat of Chedorlaomer and the kings who were with him. Then Melchizedek king of Salem brought out bread and wine; he was the priest of God Most High. And he blessed him and said:

"Blessed be Abram of God Most High,
Possessor of heaven and earth;
And blessed be God Most High,

Who has delivered your enemies into your hand."
And he gave him a tithe of all. Now the king of Sodom said to
Abram, "Give me the persons, and take the goods for yourself."

But Abram said to the king of Sodom, "I have raised my hand to the LORD, *God Most High, the Possessor of heaven and earth, that I will take nothing, from a thread to a sandal strap, and that I will not take anything that is yours, lest you should say, 'I have made Abram rich' – except only what the young men have eaten, and the portion of the men who went with me: Aner, Eshcol, and Mamre; let them take their portion."* (Genesis 14:9, 11-24 NKJV).

It is amazing, in the natural, that Abraham went after Lot when he was told of Lot's capture because, naturally, one small band of fighting men, numbering around 300, would never have defeated this army the kings had created by banding together. Each of the kings, coming from a place similar to Sodom which is described in scripture as a city, would certainly have gathered more than 300 men. So the total number of the combined army that Abraham faced, with these kings each having their own army, would probably have been over 2000 fighting men.

It could only have been with the faith of YHVH that Abraham was prepared to go after Lot. It was effectively laying his life down for his brother's son, *"Greater love has no man than this, that a man lay down his life for his friends"* (John 15:13).

Abraham did not try to build an alliance with any of the other kings in the area. He did not rely on man to rescue him. He neither turned back to where he came from in resignation, nor sat shivering in fear, waiting for the marauders to come back and wipe out his clan as well. Abraham does not do the very human thing we might do of blaming YHVH about Lot being taken. He did not doubt the call of YHVH on his life. Abraham does not do any of the things we might do. His actions display the Law of Faith. Abraham does not doubt the call of YHVH on his life, even though the Lord could easily have decided Lot brought his fate on himself by living in Sodom, especially since Abraham was instructed by God to leave his father's house and his people to go to the place God would show him. Taking Lot in the first place was outside of the Lord's instructions. It is easy to think when we have made a mistake or sowed a wrong path for our lives, that the Lord will not provide for our rescue from the situation we should never have got into in the first place. But the Lord does not do that. The Father gave Christ for us while we were still enemies separated from Him by sin (Romans 5:10).

Abraham laid down his life in the trust that the God of heaven would save him in impossible circumstances. And when the Lord gave him the victory, Abraham had the offer of alliance with the gang of war lords in exchange for the people he had gained in battle. Those kings could have attacked him and wiped him out but he refused the blood money and, instead, made covenant with Melchizedek who we know to be: *"Melchizedek, king of Salem, priest of the most high God, first being by interpretation King of righteousness, and after that also King of Salem, which is, King of peace; Without father, without mother, without descent, having neither beginning of days, nor end of life; but made like unto the Son of God; abides a priest continually"* (Hebrews 7:1-3). When the Lord gives us the victory, the spirit of this world might just think we want power, glory and money. But Abraham makes another startling decision in refusing the alliance with the murderous troop of war lords. He keeps a whole load of souls from becoming slaves to that spirit, just as Yeshua led souls in freedom from captivity through the cross.

This supernatural victory is a first mention of the Lord's taking the battle and giving us the victory that is then played out through the generations of scripture. *"Not by might, nor by power, but by my spirit, says the LORD of hosts"* (Zechariah 4:6). It is a beautiful parallel of the account when God wanted to give Gideon the victory in an impossible battle, but He did not get Gideon more fighting men. Instead, *"The LORD said unto Gideon, By the three hundred men that lapped will I save you, and deliver the Midianites into your hand"* (Judges 7:7), the same number as Abraham's army. And just as there was no doubt for Gideon that the victory had been won by the Lord, the offer of alliance made to Abraham by the war lords was scorned by Abraham in favour of the alliance he wanted to make with the priest of the God of heaven – Melchizedek. Just as in Zechariah 3, the heavenly intercession mediated the victory of the accused into imputed righteousness, so Melchizedek, the supernatural priest of heaven, is attributed by Abraham to playing such a significant role in the supernatural victory that Abraham gives Melchizedek the tithe of the spoils of that battle.

Just as Abraham would go on to obediently offer his son sacrificially, which formed a shadow for the Father to sit into in offering Yeshua for our salvation, here Abraham is laying his life down in sacrificial faith of the promises of YHVH. To lead souls to salvation in a foreshadowing of Christ's walking out the Law of Faith at the cross.

Building the Character of Faith

"Now faith is the substance of things hoped for, the evidence of things not seen" (Hebrews 11:1). Faith is the tangible reality of things that you have dreamed about but are still in vision form. Faith is always increasing. It has a never-ending life. Faith always starts somewhere but it never has a completion. The end of faith is that you believe for something, never yet seeing it, but still believing *"These all died in faith, not having received the promises, but having seen them afar off, and were persuaded of them, and embraced them, and confessed that they were strangers and exiles on the earth"* (Hebrews 11:13). When you die, you still believe you have it. That is how you get blessed because faith must increase. It is really weird because what I find is, that every time I come around the circle, faith has actually become greater. There is more responsibility and more life comes with it and I can believe for even bigger things. When you do actually see things come to pass you think, 'Wow! I can believe for that!?'

I can remember when my wife and I started our first business we were praising YHVH as He gave me a word and I saw many things in the spirit. But I did not know that He was going to break us so that we would realise our source was not in what we saw, our source of life was in who He is.

The breaking was to develop our character our relationship and friendship as a husband and wife so that we could walk through the hard knocks of life and come out the other side in a completely different way to the way we were before. *"Older men are to be sober, serious, sensible, and sound in faith, love, and endurance. Likewise, older women are to show their reverence for God by their behavior"* (Titus 2:2-3 ISV). It is that particular experience that empowered me with faith to believe for some of the things that are going on right now. It began twenty-five years ago in the strife, struggle and the turmoil of life, walking these things out. It all builds character. *"The fruit of the Spirit is love, joy, peace, longsuffering, gentleness, goodness, faith"* (Galatians 5:22). Character becomes a foundation for faith to sit on because then, it becomes not only your character, but displays the character of YHVH. Remember, everything about faith is also about the character of YHVH because He cannot fail His own character. In Him are all things. So when we have all faith, believing in all things (1 Corinthians 13:7), then we have an aspect of the character of YHVH. *"If you can believe, all things are possible to him that believes"* (Mark 9:23). We must walk through this paradox of believing yet never seeing because it is supposed to be building our character. Even though we do not see it, we still believe for it That is the issue. *"...blessed are those who have not seen and yet have believed"* (John 20:29).

It is the same with me in some of my physical experience. For ten years I walked around every day on a pain scale of six to ten out of ten. Most people do not have any idea what that means. I would come home from work, sit down for two and a half hours to get my pain level down enough so that I could lie down in bed and try to sleep. People did not know. *"To keep me grounded and stop me from becoming too high and mighty due to the extraordinary character of these revelations, I was given a thorn in the flesh..."* (2 Corinthians 12:7 VOICE). I stood on my feet for sixteen hours a day in conferences, teaching while in an extreme level of pain. I would get home and sit on the couch saying, "YHVH, I believe You. I make a choice to believe that

You are going to heal me. And if You do not, then one day I will get it fixed." I gave Him ten years. He did not heal it in ten years and so I had it fixed.

Does that destroy my faith? No, it does not. I would not trade going through that experience because of what it taught me to do in the middle of the pain. It taught me to turn into Him, to believe for something that seems absolutely impossible. And for me, personally, it has given me a tenacity that enables me to engage with something and not let it go. I am determined to hold onto that thing until I see it come to pass. That is what faith does. Faith unlocks this potential for YHVH to do things in our lives. It does not happen just because you see results. It happens when you do not see results and you still believe. When you pray for someone and you see them healed, "*Whoah!* Glory to Yeshua!" But when you pray for ten others and they do not get healed, that produces character. It produces something inside of you that just says, '*No*! I am never, never, never giving up. I am going to engage this until it is done because I know one day it is going to unlock.' Faith requires us to do that.

We tap into the law of faith:

1) By praying and spending time praying about it. You need to build a pathway. Everything in the spirit world is about building a pathway. When I was a kid in South Africa, we used to live in a place called Kloof about 20 miles outside of Durbin. At that stage there was quite a lot of wild country. I never used to understand why the local people would walk along a pathway that would zigzag. They would walk 25 metres instead of going in a straight line that was only 5 metres. But because the path was there, they would just walk along it.

We were really naughty and we would was dig a different path. Shift the grass, dig it out, and cover the beginning part of the old path. People would walk up to it and start walking along the new path. Eventually that would become their path. The old one would grow grass and you could not see it any more. We did not have TV so this is what we used to do.

Now I understand the principle of a pathway. What we need

to understand is that, when you spend time praying into this, you are building a pathway of access to the law of faith so that when you need it, it is there. The Bible says, *"Always be ready to give a [logical] defense to anyone who asks you to account for the hope and confident assurance [elicited by faith] that is within you"* (1 Peter 3:15 AMP). If you have built a path, at any given instant you can release that Glory and mandate it into a meeting, into the life of a person or into anything.

It used to frustrate me when I was a younger Christian, as there was this guy who knew about the law of faith. We went to an outreach at Western Springs in Auckland New Zealand. We had this oven in the cookhouse. It was the only oven there and it would not work. This guy said, "That's no problem Ian we will just pray for it and it will go". I thought, 'yeah right!' He laid hands on the oven, turned it on and it worked. I thought, 'Wow! what is this?!"

We spent the whole week cooking on this oven. At the end of the week we went to the manager and told him that the oven had not been working. He said, "yes I know and all the fuses have blown and it is unplugged from the wall". Now you explain that! We told him we had been cooking on it all week – what a testimony to the guy! He thought we had fixed it. He pulled the oven out and it was still unplugged and still had no fuses in it. This is the law of faith operating. It changes everything.

One day I met a man through a circumstance that was not very nice. After he went home, I felt the Holy Spirit prompt me to give him a call. I called him and went around to his place. Because of what had happened, he had taken a bottle of sleeping tablets. When I went to his house, he was barely able to stay awake. I walked up to him, plugged into the law of faith and immediately the affect of the tablets was broken off him. This is the law of faith working. It has nothing to do with my faith. It has everything to do with the higher law operating out of the Kingdom realm that has the highest set of principles where the mandate of the government sits in that thing. When that operates it changes everything.

2) You need to believe. You need to build faith for it. Faith means laying the foundation of dreaming, like: I wonder what it is going to be like to plug into that and lay hands on someone who is dead? I used to dream about walking around the supermarket and shopping mall with my cart, standing in an aisle, waiting to reach the counter and drawing on the glory of God and having everyone fall under the glory around me. What a testimony that would be, having everybody healed. You dream to operate out of the law of faith. So I walk around the supermarket now and I see a door, and I walk towards it. My family start laughing, as they know what is going on: It is not a door in the physical but the spiritual.

3) By faith, confession and by speaking the Word of God. "Father, I thank You for the law of faith that lives in the realm of your Kingdom. Today I tap into that law and I draw it around me like a covering, like a blanket. I encase myself in law of faith". It is a simple process.

4) By fasting. Spend time fasting with one objective: to engage the law of faith, so you can begin to operate in that arena.

Faith is one of the key ingredients of the tree of life that needs to grow inside our life. It only comes out of relationship with the presence of YHVH. If you do not have a relationship, the law will still operate but sometimes it will burn you because your conductors are not set to handle the 400,000 volts that comes out of the Kingdom. If you are only set to handle 250 volts, it will fry your transistors. That is a good thing because that is how you learn to change.

Activation

Father, today in Jesus Name, I acknowledge that I am under a higher law: the law of faith. Today, Lord, in Jesus Name, by faith in the Son of God, I tap into the government of the law of faith. I draw on it and I draw it around my life so that it would become a canopy and a place for You to brood over, in and around my life.

Father I ask that, as I go through life and I build an engagement with the law of faith, that You would give me opportunities and open doors for me to see this happen. Lord, I want to raise the dead. I want to do the signs and wonders on the earth and in heaven that You said I would have in this day (John 14:12). Today, I receive that from You in Yeshua's Name. Amen

Chapter 3

Faith, Hope, Desire and Truth

Before we look at faith, hope, desire and truth, I need to address an issue that people often misunderstand: assumed spiritual responsibility in contrast to delegated spiritual responsibility. We can assume spiritual responsibility, but whether we have been delegated to that spiritual responsibility is a completely different arena. Responsibility is measured by our maturity. Maturity is the key here. Maturity in our character is the anchor that engages faith, hope, desire and truth. Character is represented by the thumb of our hand. It engages all these other four which are represented by our four fingers. Without the character supporting these, you can desire all things, you can hope all things, you can have faith for all things, you can know the truth about all things, but unless you have the character to support all of it, it is useless. *"(Love)… Bears all things, believes all things, hopes all things, endures all things"* (1 Corinthians 13:7). Character is founded on love. All of these, faith, hope, desire, and truth, are intrinsically connected one with the other. You cannot just have one and assume that you have the others. The others must function together in everything you do. Character becomes a key, the trunk that holds all of these things together.

Since my teachings became available, people think they have a little bit of knowledge and that they can immediately go and put into practice all that I have taught. I am giving you a hope that there is more to this Christian life, than what you have been doing for years. I sat for five minutes with a Bible college lecturer once, who had many letters after his name. I simply quoted scripture to him. At the end of our conversation he said to me, "I need to go home and get born again. You have just undone many things that I believed about what I thought was the truth. You just unzipped it." I only quoted scripture to him, he did not even ask a question. That alone, just totally unzipped his belief system. The reason I do that kind of thing with people who are mature is so that they can go home and begin to get on their face before YHVH to build their character to handle change, especially if they have responsibility for others' lives. It is only character that teaches us how to handle responsibility for others. Everything comes back to character. Character is ground out in relationship with other people, not only just people who affirm you and say they love you, but the people who actually do not like you. It is also through conflict like this that character is built.

I know a group of young people that have been walking with YHVH, engaging in what I have been teaching and doing wonderful things together in disciplining one another. A church leader told them that they were in deception. When these types of experiences happen, it becomes an opportunity to build character. Either you know what you know and have walked with it and are affirmed in it, or it is just knowledge and if so, you can easily get blown over when someone comes along and challenges you. The Bible talks about people like that in the book of Jude: *"These are… clouds they are without water, carried about by winds; trees whose fruit withers, without fruit, twice dead, plucked up by the roots; Raging waves of the sea, foaming out their own shame; wandering stars, to whom is reserved the blackness of darkness forever"* (Jude 1:12-13). Once you know something and have truly experienced it, no one can take it away. It does not matter what goes on around you, or who says what, because you know what you know.

The law of sowing and reaping

I love the fact that YHVH vindicates you when you understand maturity and responsibility. He vindicates you because your character has been and is being developed. He really does. I excessively dislike seeing what happens to people when they engage with others who do and say things that are contrary to the Kingdom of God which derails them from their walk with YHVH. A couple of years later you see them in a mess. I hate seeing that. Our responses are so important and create a path for us that has evident fruit, but not always necessarily good fruit, because the law of sowing and reaping has taken effect. I have witnessed it taking only a couple of years for the law of sowing and reaping to be seen. We can however, continue to reap what has been sown during that time for a year, or for a decade or more depending on your responses. When we start to sow differently with the right choices, we will start to un-sow and un-reap some of that destruction caused by the wrong sowing. Some people do not see these things. Everything is about responsibility and making right choices in the middle of life's circumstances. I keep teaching people that everything to do with the Kingdom of YHVH is about responsibility. It is not about just having '*shundy bundy*' spiritual experiences or goose bumps on your goose bumps. It is about responsibility, not only for your life, but for the lives of others and for the sake of the Kingdom. The measure of your maturity is the measure of your responsibility in heaven not on earth.

The issue is not whether we have arrived at our destination. The issue is: are you on the journey? The more I know, the more I realise that I do not know, and that sometimes I have also been deceived by what I thought I knew because YHVH unzips my belief systems. You might have noticed that I teach a little bit differently than I did five years ago. This is because YHVH is unzipping some of my old belief systems. Just when I thought I was so truly there, I now realise I only knew a little piece of what I thought I knew a whole lot about. This is how YHVH builds the tabernacle of your tent in the wilderness of life's experiences.

Some families living in tents in the wilderness build a tent by adding a new piece for every child that is added to the family. This brings new life and experiences with it and over the years you add new pieces. I have found that new truths and new experiences are always found in the new pieces. What you thought you knew had just been a little piece that lays the foundation for what is to come. YHVH walks His way through our lives like this, engaging us until we suddenly realise we have learned something new and say 'Ahh that was what You were trying to tell me ten years ago. I wish I had listened and understood then, it would have saved me ten years of struggle!' However it is the ten years of struggle that helps to produce the character to handle the truth. The reason you could not handle it before was that the character was not there for the truth to sit in. Our character is the framework and must not get filled with the wrong influences.

We need to understand the importance of faith, hope, desire and truth. As I said, character is represented by the thumb of the hand. Character is the trunk of the tree that lays the foundation for all of the branches to hang on so that the tree can become fruitful. Remember the function of a tree is to produce fruit. The function of fruit is to produce seed and to protect the seed that is inside the fruit. The fruit is a sign of what the tree is. An orange tree cannot produce an apple. Everything must return to the original form of that which it has come from.

Many of those that are now being born in this generation physically are spiritually the purest form of human beings that I have seen in the blending of the human gene pool on the face of the earth since Adam's day. I am referring to this present generation along with the generation of the children that are just being born. I think some of the kids that are being born now are just weird. I have friends with children that are under a year old. These kids will look at you and their eyes go right through you. I find myself feeling, 'That is my job, not yours!' When they look at me I really want to see what they are seeing. They are very different from previous generations, because, I personally believe that this is the generation that is going to see His glory in creation.

The opposite to the 'trunk' of character is a trunk of deception. Deception can also grow its own tree out of faith in something, a false hope, desire and apparent truth. You may *think* you know the truth, and you may have the desires, but they might be based on something that you do not really know. You may hope in something, and you may even think you have faith for it, without really understanding it at all. You reap what you sow in your life. When you reap chaos you will eventually recognise that you have not got the character part right so you must have deception instead. That is probably a bit harsh, but I have got to lay this reality out so that you realise that it is actually about personal responsibility. It is about your personal life with YHVH, your development and your character. This is connected to who you are in the way that you engage the Father in that place of awe and wonderment at the glory of YHVH. It is related to the realm in Him that you are already in and that you can see yourself in. You need to have a full understanding and appreciation of yourself in His realm because that is what destroys the desire for sin.

The Lord began to speak to me about faith, hope, desire and truth, and how they are all intrinsically woven and connected together. Everything is about four dimensions. You will find patterns in the Bible. Once you find a pattern, stick with it because it will reveal a truth. This is very much the case with regard to the Father's realm and our ability to move in and out of it and these four dimensions.

As a four-dimensional functional being (which we should be), having four faces, we will be able to move in and out of time and space because 'where He is so shall we be', scripture says (John 17:21). Being in the Kingdom world empowers us to move in and out of time and space, because when we are in His world we are not in time and space anymore.

Faith and Hope

There is so much teaching about faith: how to build it, what to do with it, how to culture it, and how to cultivate it. We looked at some of it in the last chapter. You can hear more of my teaching on MP3, available at www.sonofthunder.org on Faith and How to Build It.

In Hebrews 11:1, The Word says, *"Now faith is the substance of things hoped for, the evidence of things not* (yet) *seen.'* So, in my words, faith is the tangible reality of things that you have dreamed about, but are still in vision form.

Faith is one of the key ingredients of the tree of life that needs to grow inside our life. Faith, hope, desire and truth all form the tree of life around our life. Faith is one of the key ingredients in that.

The Bible says in Proverbs 13:12, *"Hope deferred makes the heart sick: but when the desire is fulfilled, it is a tree of life."* When you are hoping on something and it almost gets there, but does not quite get there, you can feel like giving up, especially if the cycle keeps recurring. We must remember that the Hebraic way is circular not linear, so actually, our response should be, *"No!* I am not going to give up, because I know, that I know, that I know.

Hope is a really interesting substance of the tree of life. It believes all things, but does not know all things. Hope believes the possibilities, but does not look at the impossibilities. Hope engages with you to understand, but does not have all understanding with it. YHVH engages with you in hope, to begin by faith, to believe something that is not yet evident. The Word says, in Hebrews 11:1, *"Now faith is the substance of things hoped for, the evidence of things not seen."* Faith is a spiritual substance that becomes the building block for materialising what you hope for. Faith is the substance of heaven's provision. It is not seen with the naked human eye. It is seen in the world of YHVH, because YHVH paints the picture of the possibility of what can be. Then your hope must be set on that pictured possibility. One of the reasons the Father asked Israel to make things according to very specific patterns was because He was trying to teach them that there is something in heaven that looks like that. He gave specific instructions about building the temple and the candlestick to Moses. To Noah He gave specific instructions on how to build the ark. It was to give them a hope of a pattern out of heaven, that when they would come into *this* on earth, and understand it, then they would be able to enter into *that* in *heaven.* Hope is supposed to produce rest, because hope is not based on your abilities and your provision. Scripture says, "Yes, my soul, find rest in God; my hope comes from him" (Psalm 62:5). Hope is based on something that is outside of what you can do yourself and is only based on the actual substance of YHVH .

I am looking forward to the day when the full reality of who we really are and what we are really called to be becomes evident. YHVH is giving us the ability to frame a testimony, an unseen reality into life, through our words. To be able to build, but never having to labour with our hands ever again to produce a building. We simply breathe everything into existence. *"For I am the LORD your God, who stirs up the sea so that its waves roar – the LORD of hosts is His name. I have put My words in your mouth and have covered you with the shadow of My hand, to establish the [renewed] heavens and lay the foundations of the [renewed] earth, and to say to Zion (Jerusalem), 'You are My people"* (Isaiah 51:15-16 AMP). All I know is that when we get to understand who we really are in the Father, positioned in Him, when we are in that perspective looking down, all this looks completely different. The problem is we have rarely been taught we can be there looking down. We are often taught we have to be here always trying to look up. This is not the way the Father I believe wants it. The Word says we are seated in Him, high above all of these things: *"And has raised us up together, and made us sit together in heavenly places in Christ Jesus"* (Ephesians 2:6). This means that we can see things that we cannot normally see because we have a completely different perspective from a completely different view point.

Hope gives us a completely different perspective on the things that are around us so we can see them with a completely different eye. When we see this difference, we will be able frame it differently from the way it is currently framed around our life today. Hope becomes an anchor for the soul, because it is the material substance of heaven. *"Which hope we have as an anchor of the soul, both sure and steadfast, and which enters into that within the veil"* (Hebrews 6:19). Hope in faith empowers us to take what we do not see and materialise it. This is firstly achieved by dreaming. It unlocks the possibility of framing something out from the unseen world that was not there before. Building from the atomic structure that is in the universe and materializing it from the pattern of our dreaming and then being able to materialise it into substance, *"Now faith is the substance of things hoped for, the evidence of things not seen"* (Hebrews 11:1).

Desire

The Bible says that desire, when it is formed, becomes a tree of life. Proverbs 13:12: *"Hope deferred makes the heart sick: but when the desire is fulfilled, it is a tree of life."* Now, the things that we desire have to be based on the desires of the Father. The Bible says, *"Delight yourself in the LORD; and He shall give you the desires of your heart"* (Psalm 37:4). He gives them to us because our desires are supposed to be engaged in what we know in Him. When we see Him, and we see who we are there, our desires can be set upon engaging what we have seen there, in order for it to be fully revealed down here. But if your desires are set on something that is different from all we see there and based on you having a good life, or a self-centered life here then your desires will become a snare for you. When we have to hold on, especially when there is no evidence of what you are believing for and desiring, I have found that YHVH uses this in order to build our character. I am not saying, that I am any better than you. I am just saying we need to set our desire in the right place and allow the Father to unlock it for us, because when you desire a good thing the Father will unlock it for, you especially when it is in His heart and you have seen it.

If you desire something and you are at the center of it, so that it becomes the idol, YHVH may grant you the desire, but with it will come fire to break the deception. When people tell me that they so desire to be in ministry, I talk about desiring Yeshua first, dying in the church first, serving another person's ministry first, serving someone else first. All this is important. Faith, hope, desire and truth are all inter-linked. Desire is also based on your dreams. I do not mean vain fantasies when I talk about dreaming. They are not the desire of YHVH. People say, "Oh, I am just desiring to be over here and doing this and doing that." Good on you, but you might find that it never comes to pass. When YHVH has given you a desire, He triggers you about relationship: relationship with Him, intimacy, connection, yearning, about all those things associated with intimacy and relationship. The reason He does this is because once you get to know someone, then you can understand their desires. Until you get to know someone, you do not really know what their desires are. You can only assume you know.

You can read an autobiography of a person but that does not mean you know them. You only know about them. The Bible is an autobiography that teaches you *about* Him. But it is not until I come face to face, and look into His eyes that I actually realise there is a person in there. A transition must take place from knowing about someone, to knowing the person. This is so the desire of the Father can be formed in you by knowing what His desires are. In this way, He becomes the one that helps unlock your scroll. Then desire will become a tree of life and produce fruit of its own within your life and circumstances so that you can eat good fruit from your life. Faith, hope, desire and truth, will in the end, each become a tree life in their own way. Each one becomes a thumb and an anchor then having four branches each. Everything is interlinked. Once you know what the Father's heart for your life is, then you can begin to dream about what that would be like here. This will in turn begin to unlock the potential for the framework for its materialisation around your life. Once the framework is materialised, then your voice and your breath can fill it. Until you have the framework do not try and fill it, because it will get shaken out by others and run all over the place, through the holes in your character, achieving nothing, even if it weirdly makes you look good, until no one is going to relate to what you are doing, not even the Father. We want the materialising of the Father's glory in the face of the earth.

One of my desires (and I know it is in the Father's heart) is to have a fountain of the river of the glory of YHVH visible in the land of the living (Isaiah 66:12). I desire that the light of the glory of the countenance of Christ would be seen in the physical world that is around us (2 Corinthians 4:6). So, when we stand up to preach there is a visible fountain that is flowing. Instead of hearing someone talking, they will all just be looking at the fountain and being taught by the fountain, because the fountain is the river of the voice of YHVH to His people. That is why the Bible says, *"... and they shall be all taught of God"* (John 6:45). I dream about these types of things all the time and often wonder what it would be like to actually stand up in a meeting and have all of heaven begin to invade around us and shine out of us. Then our existence would be to become a fountain of the River in which everyone is hearing themselves being taught by YHVH, instead of everyone hearing the same thing that everyone else is hearing.

You have got to dream about these things to give it some foundation to work with. You need to realise that, in reality, you are not the only one standing here. I want to stretch you a bit now. Are you in YHVH? Am I in YHVH? So if all of you are in YHVH, and I am in YHVH, then I am in all of you, and all of you are in me, and we are in all of them, and they are in all of us. That we might be one with Him as He is one with the Father, as they are one with the Father. *"That they all may be one; as you, Father, are in me, and I in you, that they also may be one in us... the glory which you gave me I have given them; that they may be one, even as we are one: I in them, and you in me, that they may be made perfect in one... that the love with which you have loved me may be in them, and I in them"* (John 17:21-23, 26). So, when we become one with the Father, we are all in the Father. Therefore, all of those that are in the Father are all in us, so we fulfill "all in all". The Bible talks about, the "all in all" in 1 Corinthians 15:28: *"then shall the Son also himself be subject unto him that put all things under him, that God may be all in all."* Ephesians 4:6 says, *"One God and Father of all, who is above all, and through all, and in you all."*

So, what happens if you are a fountain of the "all in all"? Who else is going to be speaking? These are the kind of things I think about. I wonder what that would be like: Moses, Elijah, Jeremiah, Enoch. We are all in Him. These are concepts that we try to get to grips with, but it is not always easy, because often we have not allowed our brain to expand to the measure of YHVH. Paul says, *"Let this mind be in you, which was also in Christ Jesus"* (Philippians 2:5). He is talking about the full potential of all of that being fully revealed in all of this. That is what happened with Adam. When YHVH breathed into Adam he became a perfect reflection of Himself. That is why the Bible says, *"Let us make man in our image, after our likeness"* (Genesis 1:26). Desire is very important for us.

Truth

"Thus says the LORD; Cursed be the man that trusts in man, and makes flesh his arm, and whose heart departs from the LORD. For he shall be like the shrub in the desert, and shall not see when good comes; but shall inhabit the parched places in the wilderness, in a salt land which is not inhabited" (Jeremiah 17:5-6). Basically, what YHVH is saying here is, "Hey, if you trust in man you are going to find yourself in a rather unlikeable place."*"For he shall be like the shrub in the desert, and shall not see when good comes."* It is amazing how some of the church is so caught in their belief systems (because of self-idolatry) that they do not see the good that is coming. That is what is happening when people are looking at the earth saying, "Oh, the three blood moons are coming and the world is going to die!" It is because their heart is in a parched land. Remember, I said that I believe we are still here in the year 2057. *"Blessed is the man that trusts in the Lord, and whose hope the Lord is. For he shall be as a tree planted by the waters, and that spreads out her roots by the river, and shall not see when heat comes, but her leaf shall be green; and shall not be careful in the year of drought, neither shall cease from yielding fruit. The heart is deceitful above all things, and desperately wicked: who can know it? I the Lord search the heart, I try the reins, even to give every man according to his ways, and according to the fruit of his doings"* (Jeremiah 17:7-10).

Truth gives YHVH the reins of your life so that He can try your life and train it to make it His own. Having truth on the inward parts means truth about who you are, not what you want other people to think you are. It is truth about what is going on inside your life. *"Behold, you desire truth in the inward parts: and in the hidden part you shall make me to know wisdom"* (Psalm 51:6). One of the things that we need to deal with is what is going on inside our heart, things like: "I dislike you excessively!" "I do not like your shirt today." Many years ago I had to go through a situation in church life. I talk about it and the way of the cross in my book Realms of the Kingdom Volume 1 in the chapter "The Dark Cloud". If you have not known the way of the cross you need to read this.

I can remember having to go through a circumstance in which the person whose hand I was shaking had said things behind my back. I knew word for word what they had said, because I had been back and seen it in the spirit. They did not know I was there, as I had not told them. I had to deal with my own offense and the injustice. We must have truth on the inward parts because truth forms character. The Bible says, *"And ye shall know the truth, and the truth shall make you free" (John 8:32)*. The Word says when you *know* the truth. Not when you *hear* about it. Knowing means your inner man has come to the full revelation of it. Not the outside man, it is the inner man. If YHVH is all truth, then the only way to come into truth is to see Him. That is why the pure in heart shall see YHVH, because truth purifies your heart. *"Blessed are the pure in heart: for they shall see God"* (Matthew 5:8).

Faith, hope, desire and truth

Faith, hope, desire and truth become the branches that set up the four sides or facets of your operation as a functional son within creation. These four branches form four corners, with character being in the middle as the trunk functioning through these four things. Actually, they form a cube, because your whole life is based around a cube. This is because you are part of a building. You are a stone fitly joined together to the Corner Stone, forming part of a building. All of us are a cube. *"Jesus Christ himself being the chief corner stone; In whom all the building fitly framed together grows unto a holy temple in the Lord: In whom you also are built together for a habitation of God through the Spirit" (Ephesians*

2:20-22). We are a cube so that we may know the height, the depth, and the breath of our calling in Christ.

These four things (faith, hope, desire and truth) empower us to know the height, the depth and the breadth of our calling. *"That Christ may dwell in your hearts by faith; that you, being rooted and grounded in love, May be able to comprehend with all saints what is the breadth, and length, and depth, and height; And to know the love of Christ, which passes knowledge, that you might be filled with all the fullness of God"* (Ephesians 3:17-19).

Activation

Holy Spirit we want to thank You for Faith, Hope, Desire, and Truth. Lord we thank You and ask that You would engage with us as we read these pages to reveal the truth of who we are based on Your character. Holy Spirit we ask that You would reveal to us the *ways* and the *purposes* of the Father for our lives, and that these two would become an arc opening up a window for YHVH to come into us and an open window into heaven that we might go into Him. We ask this in the Name of Yeshua MaHashiach. Hallelujah! Amen!

Chapter 4
Abigail's Priestly Precedent

I have struggled to get to grips with the teaching in the body of Christ about us being a priest of God (both for men and women) for a long time. I had been trying to find an answer and it came as I was listening to Danielle Ellinas teach about Abigail from chapter 25 of 1 Samuel.

One principle in the Bible is the law of first mention. I had been looking for an Old Testament precedent that could help us understand teaching in the New Testament about us being priests. I had read the story of Nabal and Abigail many times, but suddenly, reading it again, I found my answer.

"And... (Abigail)... fell before David on her face" (1 Samuel 25:23). This is a complete surrender to a higher form of government. Here is a woman who has seen the king already in action and knows this government. The only way to come into unity with YHVH and to bring the blessing of YHVH is to actually lay down before a higher form of government. She sets the precedent here for us to lay down before a higher form of government.

"And fell at his feet, and said, Upon me, my lord, upon me let this iniquity be: and let your handmaid, I pray you, speak in your audience, and hear the words of your handmaid. Let not my lord, I pray you, regard this man of Belial, even Nabal: for as his name is, so is he; Nabal is his name, and folly is with him: but I your handmaid saw not the young men of my lord, whom you did send. Now therefore, my lord, as the LORD lives, and as your soul lives, seeing the LORD has held you back from coming to shed blood, and from avenging yourself with your own hand, now

let your enemies, and they that seek evil to my lord, be as Nabal. And now this blessing which your handmaid has brought unto my lord, let it even be given unto the young men that follow my lord…"Yet a man has risen to pursue you, and to seek your soul: but the soul of my lord shall be bound in the bundle of the living with the LORD your God; and the souls of your enemies, them shall he sling out, as out of the middle of a sling. And it shall come to pass, when the LORD shall have done to my lord according to all the good that he has spoken concerning you, and shall have appointed you ruler over Israel" (1 Samuel 25:24-27, 29-30 emphasis mine).

This woman has a major revelation about her mediation between the Ruler and a ruler, (my LORD and my lord). She is standing between them both and creating an arc between them so that reconciliation can come.

One of the biggest things that you and I have got to get to grips with is the function of our priesthood. Here is a woman setting a precedent as a precedent for kingly priesthood in the Old Testament – she is a *priest "And you shall be unto me a kingdom of priests, and a holy nation. These are the words which you shall speak unto the children of Israel"* (Exodus 19:6). She sets the precedent for you and me to be a *"priest" (yeehaw priesthood includes women).*

She goes to David and says, "Upon me, my lord…let not my lord…now therefore, my lord, as the Lord…when the Lord… to my Lord…." Can you see what she is doing? Earth to heaven; heaven to earth. She is framing a testimony to bring complete reconciliation for something that was going to be absolutely disastrous for everyone.

She had to have come to the point of being willing to die. David is not coming to play tiddlywinks, he is coming with his men to kill her husband and wipe out *every* man of Nabal's family lineage. But when David comes, this woman goes down and falls on her face at his feet and she addresses him, "My lord." The moment she says that she establishes the form of government that has a precedent on the earth to bring mercy. She was mediating mercy.

This woman thinks her husband is an animal, (or not so good), and everybody around him thinks likewise. She has this group of people and she knows that if she becomes the mediator she can spare the whole lot of them. That sounds so much like Jesus. Jesus became our mediator to spare the whole lot of us. Here in the Old Testament is this woman who, I believe, saw something in the spirit realm and engaged with it actively. YHVH set a precedent there for you and me to show us how to mediate between heaven and earth. I am not just talking about women here, I am talking about being a priest.

In the Old Testament, the example of priesthood was of a priest going into the Holy of Holies once a year. But other people had no right to even refer to the Name of the Lord in heaven. That right was given only to the priests in the temple because they considered it so holy. Abigail had no right to take the Name of the Lord out into the marketplace, out into the middle of an army coming to engage and destroy their town, their city and the men in their nation. She had no right whatsoever to actually bring His name into the marketplace. For that alone she should have been killed. But this woman saw something and was engaged in something that was way beyond her time. She set a precedent for you and me by teaching us how to engage in mediation as a priest in *our* day. You too are supposed to mediate between heaven and earth as a priest. Jesus has set the example.

In the Old Testament, you find that the priest would go in once a year. He would have to go through the veil. But David uncovered something that was so precious and so amazing that he did not need a veil. This woman had seen that and was now engaging David in the position of a king to mediate without a veil because she set herself and said, "Here is my lord. Let the LORD..." You could not say the name of YHVH, (and I will not even say His holy name), we do not even know the correct pronunciation of the secret name of God. They would not even write "*the Name*", instead they substituted the letters YHVH which is now translated with the capital letters LORD in some English Bibles. This is not God's name. It is what He is *called*, but it is not His Name. Unless you are a Messianic priest you will not even know what His secret name is. Yet here is a woman, who knows the secret name of God, and she says,

"My lord, David to my LORD in heaven". So she stands to be killed, not only by David, but by YHVH who is in heaven. *"You shall not take the name of the LORD your God in vain; for the LORD will not hold him guiltless that takes his name in vain"* (Exodus 20:7). She is mediating reconciliation between the corruption of sin in her family line and in her town: and she is mediating with *a man* so that YHVH would be glorified.

This is what blows me away: *"Then David sent word to Abigail, asking her to become his wife"*, (1 Samuel 25:39). The previous verse had said, *"...the LORD struck Nabal and he died."*

Do you realise that it is not until you have mediated as a priest for God that He will come and espouse you to Himself? We teach about the bride but it is not about wearing white, fluffy dresses. Abigail's name means "the Father's joy, and the Father's delight." The church has taught about being a bride but the precedent is to become a priest. *"...as the bridegroom rejoices over the bride, so shall your God rejoice over you"* (Isaiah 62:5), *"But you are a chosen generation, a royal priesthood, a holy nation, a people for his own"* (1 Peter 2:9). *"For I am jealous over you with godly jealousy: for I have espoused you to one husband, that I may present you as a chaste virgin to Christ"* (2 Corinthians 11:2).

I believe the Old Testament high priest would get drawn in through the veil. It was a solid piece of material and when the high priest approached, YHVH would breathe him in, and he would begin to disassemble in his molecular structure and actually go through the material of the curtain and rematerialise on the other side of the veil. The veil was not torn in those days. I also believe that when the high priest arrived on the other side of the veil, before the Holy of Holies, that the second day in creation would actually open up. So he could stand in the very beginning and mediate from the beginning *before* second creation sin came into being.

We might think of the Holy of Holies as a trans-dimensional gate, a vehicle to shift the high priest all the way back to the very beginning, where there was no record of sin in any form whatsoever. The high priest would exchange, at the beginning, *all* of the sin, *all* of the sin of Israel, for complete holiness. Then he would come back from the very beginning, back into the Holy of Holies. The moment he would arrive back in the Holy of Holies, a divine exchange had been completed where he had mediated the sin of six million people (estimated). We struggle with our *own* sin because we have not been taught that we can go in. We can go back to the beginning and we can bring the beginning back into our day so there is no record of sin. But it is Old Testament protocol: here is a woman who shows she has seen something in the future because she sings songs about David. The Bible says very clearly that all the women sang these songs, (1 Samuel 18:6-7). This woman had seen something in the future and she applies it to her day. She brings the experience of our day into her day by mediating reconciliation for the sin of her family; to bring it to a point where her family is completely released because of her mediating and saying: "I have sinned."

Nehemiah saw exactly the same thing and then did exactly the same thing that she did. Nehemiah said, "I have sinned", (when he may not have sinned as they had). "I have sinned. I and all my Father's generations have sinned against You. Today I am taking responsibility. I am going to mediate restitution and restoration for all of my generational line. Instead of saying, "*your* sin" has caused Israel to be broken down, Jerusalem's walls to be broken down and her gates displaced, he says, "That is *my* sin."

"... hear the prayer of your servant, which I pray before you now, day and night, for the children of Israel your servants, and confess the sins of the children of Israel, which we have sinned against you: both I and my father's house have sinned" (Nehemiah1:6).

Nehemiah mediated for that sin before the Father. So the Father brought complete restoration and restitution to the whole city of Jerusalem through one person becoming a priest who was not a priest. Nehemiah was not actually a priest. None of these men that we read about in the Old Testament were priests except Aaron and his family and yet they all did priestly things. It fries your brain when you see what they do.

We find Abigail mediating like this and due to her *humility* and *vulnerability*, God is able to mediate something in the spirit realm to bring restoration not only to them, but to their family line. "If you sin against someone, God can help [intercede/mediate/arbitrate for] you" (1 Samuel 2:25 EXB).

Do you realise that when we as husbands and wives become vulnerable to one another like that we begin to mediate complete restoration to our family line? That is why some of our families are in such a mess. It is because this restoration has not happened yet between husband and wife. I am not saying you are responsible for it. I am just saying there is a possibility that you have not mediated something there yet.

New Testament

In the New Testament, within the Order of Melchizedek, the functionality of sonship is expressed via a tree comprised of four branches: king, priest, oracle and legislator, (sonship is the trunk of this tree.) Abigail did all of these four things. She represented herself and her husband, putting herself in a position of complete vulnerability to become a *priest.* She used words (*oracle*) to create an atmosphere that David could position himself in as a ruler (*king),* to release forgiveness so that she could then begin to mediate legislation (*legislator*).

This woman is behaving and mediating as a New Testament priest. In the Old Testament, women were not allowed in the Holy of Holies or even anywhere near it in Jerusalem. But she tapped into something of the Kingdom realm that was beyond her years and her understanding because she wanted to serve the Lord.

That is why she said, "My lord!" Do you think she was talking to David? She was, but she was speaking to the power Source *behind* him. So she was saying, "My lord...to my Lord, my lord...to my Lord." What she was doing was reconciling these two together (David and YHVH) because, in government, decisions are made for liberty on the *earth.* If you see a person and do not see when YHVH is behind the person, you are going to miss the person's significance.

Abigail saw something: "My lord, my Lord." David was not

king yet, so David had no right to be called *lord.* So why was she calling him *lord*? Because he was powerful? Perhaps, but actuall I believe she was acknowledging the *Power* that was behind David. She recognized in David the source of all he was doing and that his complete ability was the power of the Someone that stood behind him. She recognized the source of the government that sat on David and then she reconciled David and Nabal together; and also reconciled David to YHVH by surrendering herself and making herself completely vulnerable.

You and I have to learn how to mediate like this on the earth today. To be priests we need to learn from scripture like this and follow what this woman did in mediating reconciliation. To a Hebrew, *repentance* is not about saying "I am sorry, I am sorry..." That is Greek thinking. For a Hebrew, there are five steps to repentance. To Hebrews the final engagement with repentance is *turning* towards the face of YHVH. It means turning to the state of complete awe and wonderment of who YHVH is in heaven, who you are in Him and who He is in you. That is repentance to a Hebrew. It has nothing to do with saying "I am sorry, sorry, sorry, forgive me Jesus." The issue is, when you turn and you go there, you are already forgiven.

A priest has got to take the first step to mediation. That is why she sent her servants and the gifts – because you have got to bring an offering to the Lord. So it says in the Old Testament, "Bring your *tithes* and *offerings* into the house" (Malachi 3:10). Well, the New Testament is about *gifts* and *giving.* The Old Testament says *you* own it and you give Him ten percent. In the New Testament, the truth is that He owns it all. You ask Him how much you keep.

Abigail brought an offering unto the Lord to engage with *the Lord*, not with David, but also to supply David with what he needed. She recognized that an offering would break open the ground for the heart of the king to receive a word from YHVH to release *her family.*

That is why we are to offer our bodies as a living sacrifice as Paul says,

"I beseech you therefore, brethren, by the mercies of God, that you present your bodies a living sacrifice, holy, acceptable unto God, which is your reasonable service" (Romans 12:1). My teaching on being a *Living Sacrifice* can be downloaded in audio form from my website: www.sonofthunder.org and is also published in the limited edition of Realms of the Kingdom Volume 2 Trading in the heavens.

If we are not prepared to lay our life down, we will not become a priest.

We have got to lay our lives down so YHVH can engage us on the level of the dominion of priesthood. Then He can release us into our function, which is to go into the realm of heaven and begin to mediate on behalf of something that we have taken responsibility for. You cannot mediate for anything unless you have taken responsibility for it. That is why Abigail said, "Let it be on me." She had to be prepared to die.

Do you realise that the New Testament priest has also got to be prepared to die, the same as the Old Testament priest was? If his preparation in the Old Testament was not to the extent that he was fully whole and fully clean when he went in there, he would be killed. So he had to be prepared to die.

In the same way *she* was prepared to die because she had learned that there is *'a priesthood from another realm'* and another time in the future. She knew that she could engage it because she knew this man David had touched it in another time and in another future. That is why he could do amazing things. I personally think they talked about the things that David did in Israel, especially since the Bible quotes songs that came out, *"And the women sang to one another as they played, and said, Saul has slain his thousands, and David his ten thousands"* (1 Samuel 18:7). This means the 'bush-telegraph' was working really well.

Abigail presented herself before David, bringing gifts and bringing an offering to the Lord, because actually YHVH wants your life. As a New Testament priest, you have got to be prepared to give your life anytime you become a priest to mediate for something on the face of the earth. You have got to be prepared to die. And if you die, so be it! The issue is, are you willing? She was willing to give her life to die for something that was not her fault.

In the New Testament, you and I, as a New Testament priest, must be prepared to give our life for something that was not our fault. You must take complete responsibility for it and begin to engage it and go in before the Lord with it. Your presentation must be with surrender and submission. Doing some study on the way this woman went about what she did shows us that she opens a process up for us for today. She gathered her servants, she gathered an offering, and she brought to David *bread.*

When David went to Nabal, he was approaching a wealthy ruler. Nabal had the secret of the recipe of the showbread. David sent his men in his name to Nabal and asked him, *"Let the young men find favor in your eyes: for we come on a feast day: give, I pray you, whatsoever comes to your hand unto your servants, and to your son David",* (I Samuel 25:8). So, do you think David was asking for bread, or do you think he was asking for the priestly portion? Nabal replied, in effect, "No, it is mine." He said, *"Who is David? And who is the son of Jesse?"* (v10). But his wife recognized the priest of YHVH.

David purposefully went to engage the priestly function, *"The LORD has sworn, and will not relent, You are a priest forever after the order of Melchizedek"* (Psalm of David 110:4). To become a king, you also have to be a priest. David was anointed as a king but he had to be a priest first. He learned how to be a priest in the wilderness, playing his harp.

David's mighty men were called men of renown because they were of the seed-line mentioned in Genesis, *"The sons of God came in unto the daughters of men, and they bore children to them, the same became mighty men which were of old, men of renown."* When the sons of God came to earth, they came *in unto* the daughters of men. They did not *take* them away as in verse 2 when *"the sons of God saw the daughters of men that they were fair; and they took them wives of all which they chose"* (Genesis 6:4 emphasis mine).

David continually played his harp in the presence of these men of renown. Their DNA got re-tuned by David's connection with YHVH because he presented himself as a priest, night and day, and day and night in the cave. His men were continually within the sound of the priesthood. As a result, they got so changed by engaging with that that they became judges in Israel when David became king.

Your mediation as a priest before the presence of YHVH does not only affect you, *"But you are a chosen generation, a royal priesthood, a holy nation, a people for his own; that you should show forth the praises of him who has called you out of darkness into his marvelous light"* (1 Peter 2:9). It affects *every single person* that is in your sphere of influence. And you do not have to be the boss. David was not originally the king. David was a vagabond in the caves in Israel, busy learning how to be a priest, living out of his future, seeing our day and bringing it into his day.

Do you realise that this woman would also have to have seen this? For her to get an understanding of what she did, the Spirit of Wisdom would have to have counseled her because she knew exactly what to do when her servants came.

Most women would go to their husbands and say, "Honey, you are going to die! Let's protect ourselves!" But she decided, "No, I am not doing that...he is an idiot – busy having a *party*!" I have taught about people who hang around the hem of the glory. They are like the children of Israel who got drunk and went into idolatry making a golden calf. They have a party and they get into sin. You cannot be around the *hem* of the glory. You have to be either *in* the realm of the glory or totally out of it, but do not stand in between because you will mess your life up.

Nabal is doing *his* thing and she is out doing *her* thing. He is busy getting drunk and she is busy laying on her face, to later become a priest in front of David. I have often wondered, when I read through that passage before, what would have happened if Nabal had responded differently. I wonder what would have actually happened to Nabal and his family. An intervention of a woman saved a whole household. But imagine if *the man* had taken responsibility. I am really tired of women taking our responsibility, guys. Do you realise that most of the intercessors are women? Not all of them, but a good portion of them, and they are usually older women.

I find it so interesting that this woman became David's bride.

Once you have learned how to mediate as a priest you are going to get espoused to the one that you are mediating for. This is because the heart of the one you are mediating for turns towards you, and their eyes get fixed on you. When the eye of the Lord gets fixed on you, you are going to start to be drawn into complete union with Him *"The one who is united and joined to the Lord is one spirit with Him"* (1 Corinthians 6:17 AMP).

This woman in essence says to David, "Let it be to me; do to me; I am going to die – I am happy to die here. I am happy to die; let the judgment that you were going to put upon my husband come on me. If the judgment sits on me, then my husband can be free."

Do you realise the church is under such bondage when it is busy just having a party? I am not trying to be nasty. I am just stating a fact. We have not been taught about the humility of priesthood and all these simple things. You and I have been given jobs as New Testament priests (1 Peter 2:9), to intercede for the forgiveness of the body of Christ and to mediate the reconciliation of the body of Christ to the Father through Jesus. This is even when they do not deserve it; even though the religious system does not deserve it. Even though sometimes we are having our own little pity parties and doing our own thing in our churches.

The Father wants us to understand that there is a responsibility connected to mediation. Mediation means that you might lose your life. He wants you to understand that you are going to lose it anyway but, if you are prepared to lose it, you are going to find it. YHVH is doing some freaky things today and unlocking some freaky things for us.

I often wonder what would have happened if David had killed her. What her servant's responses would have been if David had killed her? How would David's men have responded if David had killed her himself? He had the right to. I wonder how David's men would have felt if this woman came, in her humility, to David, and David had killed her. I try and look at all these things. How would it have gone? If David killed her,

David's men would have been disgusted and would probably have left him.

When you begin to mediate like this, the presence of YHVH begins to engage with you in the spirit realm to such an extent that others will look to your leadership, even though you are not a leader. This woman was not the leader of her home but, because she took responsibility, others looked to her leadership. That is why the servants came to her with the message, "your husband is an idiot!" *"David sent messengers from the wilderness to greet our master, but he screamed insults at them"* (1Samuel 25:14 NLT). The Bible says do not tell anyone they are a fool (Matthew 5:22). Yet Abigail came to David and told him that her husband was a *fool*, or an *idiot* in today's language: *"I know Nabal is a wicked and ill-tempered man; please do not pay any attention to him. He is a fool, just as his name suggests"* (v25 NLT).

David knew something about YHVH: that in complete humility, forgiveness is given. That is why the Word says, *"Humble yourselves therefore under the mighty hand of God"* (1 Peter 5:6). We have got to humble ourselves and be prepared to die.

One of the jobs you and I are going to have as a modern day priest is to mediate the forgiveness of the body of Christ to Jesus Himself. "He said to them, "My soul is overwhelmed with sorrow to the point of death. Stay here and keep watch with me" (Matthew 26:38). Now that is quite a bit of a responsibility. But it is something we should not be afraid of but, rather, we should rejoice towards it.

When Abigail went there and laid down before David, I believe that she actually went there rejoicing because she had already let go. She had given everything that she had.

"Then Abigail made haste, and took two hundred loaves, and two skins of wine, and five sheep already dressed, and five measures of parched grain, and a hundred clusters of raisins, and two hundred cakes of figs, and laid them on donkeys" (1 Samuel 25:18).

The middle of all her offering is ten: five plus five. This woman had wisdom. She brings a kingly ransom to the king. Two hundred loaves of bread was a lot of food in those days. Actually what I believe she brought was two hundred loaves of showbread. She brought them to the king because she saw he was one that was honoured by YHVH as a priest.

Jesus our High Priest

Until we begin to engage Jesus as a priest, we will not step into our own priesthood, because we have not learned priesthood from the Priest. That is why I have been talking to the body of Christ about needing to go through the veil into the place where we actually experience Jesus as our high priest *"Seeing then that we have a great high priest, that is passed into the heavens, Jesus the Son of God, let us hold fast our profession"* (Hebrews 4:14). YHVH cannot function outside of priesthood. You have got to learn how to mediate. You cannot learn how to mediate until *you* have been mediated over. We need to learn how mediation happens. You and I need to go and present ourselves before the High Priest who is Christ, forever after the Order of Melchizedek. "Therefore, holy brethren, partakers of the heavenly calling, consider the Apostle and High Priest of our profession" Christ Jesus" (Hebrews 3:1), Jesus is the high priest of your confession and the framework of your life. We need *to yield* to YHVH in this. Abigail brings her offerings to David. She lays them down at his feet and then gives her offering willingly. For me, personally, I believe she would have had an amazing smile on her face because she was completely surrendered, thinking: 'If he kills me, he kills me.'

Esther was another woman who did that for a whole nation. She could have and should have been killed when she walked into the king's throne room unannounced (Esther 4:16). These women in the Old Testament had an awareness about being a priest. Esther came into the king in great humility at the risk of her life to mediate for her people. She prepared herself to look really gorgeous to him "...six months with oil of myrrh, and six months with perfumes, and with other preparations for beautifying women" (Esther 2:12).

Do you think that Abigail went before David adorned in a rubbishy garment? Riding on a donkey is an amazing issue for a woman. Mary rode on a donkey. Jesus rode on a donkey And

"Jesus, when he had found a young donkey, sat thereon; as it is written" (John 12:14). Many people YHVH has crowned have ridden on a donkey, especially when they are going somewhere to present themselves in a certain fashion, to reveal knowledge about the future. YHVH is about to put the Priest of Christ on a donkey, and reveal them in their priesthood.

David, in his response to her, opens up his heart to such an extent that she went on to become his bride. We must first learn mediation from Christ who is *our* Mediator, between us and God. Then as we begin to learn the function of mediation, and we begin to stand and to mediate, the Lord opens up His heart to such an extent that we come into complete union with Him.

The way you get the Father's response is by becoming a mediator for others. But it has got to start with your own. Once YHVH *unlocks* your own healing, then you can become a mediator for other people's healing. This starts at home. Husbands! Wives! This starts at home. You have got to learn how to become a mediator of those that are around you because, first *"in Jerusalem, and in all Judea, and in Samaria, and then into the uttermost part of the earth"* (Acts 1:8).

One day we are going to become a priest to the earth. Who do you think is going to reconcile the earth back into the glory of God again? *"My people, who are called by my name, will humble themselves and pray and seek my face and turn from their wicked ways, then I will hear from heaven, and I will forgive their sin and will heal their land"* (2 Chronicles 7:14) Do you realise you become a priest of your solar system because it is also in a mess, and it also needs reconciliation. You become a priest to your galaxy and to the universe because your job is to bring creative light back into all that is now dark matter. *"For the creation eagerly awaits the revelation of the sons of God... For we know that the whole creation groans together and suffers birth pains until now"* (Romans 8:19, 22 TLV). Do you know that 'out there' you are called the *'light bringers'*, the freaky ones that emanate the glory of the Creator, that bring light into the universe. That is why the Word says that we are going to shine like the stars in heaven. *"And they that are wise shall shine as the brightness of the firmament; and they that turn many to righteousness as the stars forever and ever"* (Daniel 12:3).

Do you realise also that, because of your cleansed seed line, you are going to be a reconciler, trans-dimensionally, for all of the corruption that was messed up in the other dimensional realms. Do you know that Jesus did that? The Bible says in the book of Hebrews that after Jesus died, He took His blood into the heavenly temple, and cleansed the heavenly temple from the record of sin that was there.

"So Christ has now become the High Priest over all the good things that have come. He has entered that greater, more perfect Tabernacle in heaven, which was not made by human hands and is not part of this created world. With his own blood – not the blood of goats and calves – he entered the Most Holy Place once for all time and secured our redemption forever". (Hebrews 9:11-12 NLT)

The Bible says you are going to do the same things as Jesus has done and He has left some things for us to do trans-dimensionally. If we are going to do the same things that Jesus did, we had better get prepared.

"He that believes on me, the works that I do shall he do also; and greater works than these shall he do; because I go unto my Father" (John 4:12).

Jesus took His life and engaged to such an extent that He brought reconciliation in heaven by *His* blood and that blood speaks forever. *"And to Jesus the mediator of the new covenant, and to the blood of sprinkling, that speaks better things than that of Abel"* (Hebrews 12:24). Therefore you need to understand that *your* blood, (which is going to be the blood of the Father because you are carrying His DNA), is going to speak the *same* way as Jesus' blood spoke. (See *Realms of the Kingdom Volume 1: chapter entitled the DNA of God*).

Some of us are so afraid of saying that we are going to be like our Father. This comes from the tree of the knowledge of good and evil, not the tree of life. Sometimes we are afraid that out of the *knowledge* of good and evil, we are going to make YHVH evil. I have some good news for you today: You cannot corrupt YHVH. But when you come as corrupt *to* Him, YHVH changes you to incorruption, as you put on incorruption. *"For this corruptible must put on incorruption, and this mortal must put on immortality"* (1Corinthians 15:53).

He does this because He has called us priests of our God. That means you are under a Priesthood – a priesthood you have to learn about.

"Jesus Christ, who is the faithful witness, and the first begotten of the dead, and the prince of the kings of the earth... And hath made us kings and priests unto God" (Revelation 1:5-6 KJV).

"You also, as living stones, are built up into a spiritual house, a holy priesthood, to offer up spiritual sacrifices, acceptable to God by Jesus Christ" (1 Peter 2:5 emphasis mine.)

To start learning about your priesthood you first need to go through the veil and present yourself to your High Priest. That is where you learn about how He mediates over *your* life to reconcile *you* completely out of your sin and brokenness. It is not about earning brownie points, praying twenty-five hours a day. It is about what He can do in heaven, to mediate you out of *your* sin, to bring complete reconciliation to your brokenness in heaven. Through that mediation, you can then bring the brokenness of *others.* You can mediate *their* brokenness to complete incorruption in heaven. We *must* follow the same pattern. *"Then I said, "Put a clean turban on his head." So they put a clean turban on his head and clothed him, while the angel of the Lord stood by"* (Zechariah 3:5).

David's response to Abigail through her humility was to call her his bride. He sent his *servants* to her. A king does not usually send his servants to go and say, "Hey, can you marry me?" A proposal is normally face to face. "Hi, will *you* be my wife?" You say it eye to eye, face to face, in the presence of the person. But David's servants knew so much about the heart of David, and who he was, that they came, as *his face*, to represent him. *"Then David sent word to Abigail, asking her to become his wife. His servants went to Carmel and said to Abigail, "David has sent us to you to take you to become his wife."* (1 Samuel 25:39-40). You and I have to come face-to-face with Yeshua. Then He can send us to others to be His face because we understand who He is to such an extent. This will be out of our relational connection and intimacy, out of our weaving in quantum entanglement with His presence. Only from that place can we say to others, "Will you come in? Will you become one with Me? My Master has need of you over here."

David showed us a way. The price of a ruler is not only to understand mediation as priesthood, but to give an endowment to all of those around to such an extent that they follow your heart. David's mighty men were so knitted to him that they went through enemy lines just to get him water from the well of Bethlehem.

"And David longed, and said, Oh that one would give me drink of the water of the well of Bethlehem, which is by the gate! And the three mighty men broke through the host of the Philistines, and drew water out of the well of Bethlehem, that was by the gate, and took it, and brought it to David" (1 Samuel 23:15-16).

David did some amazing things, and these men around him did some amazing things because David brought them to such a point that they had become his arm, ears and face in the community. Anything that David wanted they would go and get because David began to encompass them. The job of a king is to engage in governmental authority, high above everything else, and bring all *that* in underneath to bring *it* to maturity. Then, out of the maturity, they become an arm of your arm, an eye of your eye and a leg of your leg. That is what David did.

I have talked about you being a tree. (See my MP3 teaching: "*Growing Trees*" available on my website www.sonofthunder.org) The Bible calls us trees of righteousness in Isaiah 61:3. We are a tree, and the function of that tree is to provide an overshadowing so that whoever hides under that shadow can get brought to maturity in the full likeness of the image that is overshadowing us. *"He that dwells in the secret place of the most High shall abide under the shadow of the Almighty"* (Psalm 91:1).

In Genesis 2:9, the tree of life was in the midst of God's garden, Eden, and Genesis 3:24 refers to a *way* of the tree of life. The tree of life was a shadow that could bring Adam and Eve to full maturity. When Adam hid, he hid out from YHVH's shadow, not behind some bushes. They chose to shift themselves out from YHVH's covering and place themselves under another one called the tree of the *knowledge* of good and evil.

This brings us back to Abigail. The reason that the servants came to their mistress Abigail, was because they knew that there was something in her that empowered *her* to be able to do something that Nabal could not do. They saw a *grace* in her that empowered *her* to go way beyond because she had overshadowed those servants and protected them, therefore they loved her. You do not go to the wife of someone and say, "Your husband is an idiot" (1 Samuel 25:17) unless you know that you are loved because, actually, she had the right to kill them. But they loved *her* and they honoured *her* in who she was in that realm. I believe this woman tapped into something that was mystical here and, in engaging with it, the servants recognized that, so she came as *their* face, and then David's servants came as *his* face.

You come as a the face of Priest into heaven and then the Father presents His Son to you. "I have espoused you to one husband, that I may present you as a chaste virgin to Christ" (2 Corinthians 11:2). *You* then become His face to the world that is around you. These patterns are woven in and out of scripture. "Go and cry in the ears of Jerusalem, saying, Thus says the LORD; I remember you, the kindness of your youth, the love of your betrothal" (Jeremiah 2:2).

We have each been called to be a priest so we have got to learn to live out of that realm of eternity and the mystical realms of heaven and begin to engage in our process as sons. You and I have been called a son for a reason, because the Father is making us kings and priests. *"...Jesus Christ...the prince of the kings of the earth...loves us, and washed us from our sins in his own blood, And has made us a kingdom and priests unto God and his Father"* (Revelation 1:5-6).

Do you realise the word *"make"* is there for a reason – because actually you do not have a choice? I have got some really bad news for you. You have been yoked to something that has now started to pull you towards a destiny. Whether you like it or not, you are going to go there. You have a choice as to whether you will come out of it with full glory and full honour.

Do you realise that the watchman who came to the five wise and five foolish virgins was the priest and mediator of heaven to earth? We hear so much in the body of Christ about the five foolish virgins and the five wise virgins that we miss the significance of the watchman. The watchman was the mediator of heaven's arrival on earth and earth's arrival into heaven. The watchman was the *gate.* Do you know we become a gate? The Bible is very clear about that. You are a gate. *"Lift up your heads, O you gates"* (Psalm 24:7).

YHVH is going to unlock your mediation as a priest. You had better just get on board with it, because, if you do not, you will get dragged in there screaming, kicking, wanting to do your own thing. I would rather go like Abigail, willingly. Actually, there is not so much of a reward in getting dragged in but there is a huge reward in going there and laying your life down and saying, on your face, "I surrender, Father, to my priesthood." In this day we have got to embrace our function as a priest.

Activation

Father I want to honour the priests of God, the men and women who have made a way in the past, to be able to mediate heaven on earth, and to be able to mediate earth to heaven. Father, we want to honour them for the price they paid.

We honour the men in white linen[5] that gather in our midst. We want to honour the priests of our God and of His Christ. We honour the men of David. We honour David.

Father, we honour what You have done to show us the way to be priests. Lord we honour You today. Yeshua, we honour You for being our High Priest.

So, Father, today, by faith, we enter into the realm of Your presence. Father, by faith, we put our hands up against the veil and we walk through into the realm of Your presence.

---

[5] Men in white linen is discussed in Realms of the Kingdom Volume 2 Trading in the heavens Limited Edition, Chapter 12

Father, we stand here today as part of an ecclesia that comes and says, "Lord, we want to learn! We want to be yoked to our priesthood as a believer today."

Lord, Your Word says You have *called us*, that you have *made us* kings and priests. You have made us a kingdom of priests. Lord, today we ask that You would yoke us to our priesthood. We ask that You would begin to instruct us, teach us, and bring us into the revelation of the ability we have to bring complete restitution and reconciliation to all that is around us. Father, I ask that You would open our eyes to begin to see, our ears to begin to hear, that we would come to a point of maturity, and that You would be able to rest Your head upon us, because presently"... *the Son of man has nowhere to lay his head*" (Luke 9:58; Matthew 8:20).

Father, we ask that You would help us going forward, that You would unlock the secrets of the mystery of our priesthood in Your presence. Lord, using Abigail's life, reveal to us all that we need to do, and all that we need to know in order to understand the pattern. Father, through what Esther did, reveal the pattern. Father, through what Daniel did, unlock and reveal the pattern to us. Father, through the New Testament in what Yeshua did for us, we ask that You would empower us to see '*the pattern*'.

Then help us to be able to walk *towards* our destiny as priests. Father we turn our eyes towards that mark of the high calling in God to be a priest of our Lord, that our Lord may engage with us in *our* lordship, to present *His* Lordship to all of the earth.

Father, thank you that You called us '*lords*', that You have called us '*kings*', that You are the King of *kings* and the Lord of lords. "*And he has on his robe and on his thigh a name written, KING OF KINGS, AND LORD OF LORDS*" (Revelation 19:16). "*You are a chosen people, a royal priesthood*" (1 Peter 2:9).

Father, we yoke ourselves today, *by faith,* to our mandate to be called "*priests of God*". We yoke ourselves to that today, Father. We ask that You would *instruct* us and You would *lead* us into our destiny and into our future, as a bride. There is an invitation to become a priest, to feast at the table of our Father in heaven.

We ask this in Yeshua's wonderful name.

Father we bring this now into the atmosphere that is around us. We bring it *out* of heaven, and we bring it *into* the earth, Father, so that we now are a container for a destiny that is going to unlock heaven, to the world around us. Hallelujah!

Chapter 5
Judge Your House

And if the whole congregation of Israel sins through ignorance, and the thing be hid from the eyes of the assembly, and they have done somewhat against any of the commandments of the LORD concerning things which should not be done, and are guilty...And the priest that is anointed shall bring some of the bullock's blood to the tabernacle of meeting...so shall he do with this: and the priest shall make an atonement for them, and it shall be forgiven them (Leviticus 4:13, 16, 20).

In ancient Israel one of the things the high priest would do is to come in before the presence of YHVH and take responsibility for the total sin of everyone in the nation. That was part of his role as the high priest.

So once a year that nation, in an instant, would be totally free from every single thing that had ever gone wrong, from any iniquity, transgression or sin that they had walked in throughout the year. It would all be totally and absolutely dealt with.

The high priest would make an exchange because that is the high priest's role. Basically the high priest would stand before the Lord and say, "Here is the sin of Israel. I stand on behalf of them. This is *my* sin. This is what *I* have done."

Before mediation can happen there needs to be responsibility taken for sin. Unless there is ownership of sin, nothing can change. There can be no mediation if there is no ownership. This is one of the key things in unlocking the mediation of Christ as your High Priest, as a Mediator before the Father of our confession, *"Therefore, holy brethren, partakers of the heavenly calling, consider the Apostle and High Priest of our profession, Christ Jesus"* (Hebrews 3:1).

Let us take a look at sin. Sin is not what you do. Sin is what you are. Sin is what you have been from the foundation, when you were formed in your mother's womb. You had twenty-two pairs of autosomes and one chromosome from your father, twenty-two pairs of autosomes and one chromosome from your mother. These joined together like a *Ketubah*, or marriage contract, to form you as a human being. Those twenty-three bits from each parent form a scroll of testimony that carries a record of every single thing that your family line has ever carried, all the way back to Adam. And if you have got reptilian or different seed[6] mixed inside your family line, then it goes back even further.

Responsibility

Throughout the Bible, it is important for us to realise we need to take responsibility for our sin. If we do not take responsibility for sin, then there will be no accountability for it and no responsibility for it. There is then no mediation of anything.

So, sin is what we *are*. There is no classification for sin in the Hebrew culture. We classify it by saying something like: "Murder is really bad. But lust in the heart of a person is not so bad." We classify sin. It is Greek thinking that has classified sin as: "terrible, just a bit bad and not so bad." Yeshua tried to address it when he was speaking to the Pharisees, bringing in the message of the Kingdom saying, *"You have heard that it was said, 'YOU SHALL NOT COMMIT ADULTERY'; but I say to you that everyone who [so much as] looks at a woman with lust for her has already committed adultery with her in his heart."* (Matthew 5:27-28 AMP).

Actually sin is all about a frequency. It is the generation of the trigger inside you that performs that stuff in the spirit world. You have become a platform, and then you bear the image of that thing. So, whatever goes on inside your heart vibrates and

[6] For more teaching on this subject please refer to Realms of the Kingdom Volumes 1 and 2.

that vibration sets up a frequency, which sets a platform for that image to be born on the earth. When a spirit of murder sees its own image, it will step into that image.

People have said to me, "The devil cannot read your brain." Really? Many of us have conversations with him all the time. Familiar spirits[7] say things to you like, "They really do not like you." "No, they don't." "Man, they did not even say hello to me today!" "Yeah man, that is really bad!" "Yeah, they didn't." "That's really bad." *"And the evil spirit answered and said, Jesus I know, and Paul I know; but who are you?"* (Acts 19:16).

Have you ever had those conversations inside yourself? If you say you have not, then you may be deceived. I have found that most Christians have between five and seven familiar spirits in their mind that speak to them all the time in the first person. When your Pastor comes and does not say hello to you but shakes the hand of the person sitting right next to you, you think, 'Man, he didn't even say hello to me! That makes me feel bad. I feel really rejected.' No I don't. Yes I do.' Back and forth it goes, as we have this schizophrenic thing going on inside us.

Your thoughts are frequencies of energy and that energy displays a platform. The enemy sees the platform and he goes right into it. I have been around too many Christians and seen demons cast out of too many of them not to know that demons can live in Christians and trigger conversations inside them. Ninety-eight percent of every deliverance session I have done has been on believers. That is because the light in them drives that stuff to the surface. It happens in pastors also. At a conference I went to, there were three thousand five hundred pastors, and eight hundred of them were manifesting all at the same time. These were senior leaders of churches of one or two thousand people. They were just broken. But there is a frequency that has a shadow and an image in it. And since there has been no record of that thing actually taken into the realm of heaven and judged[8], it still sits inside the autosome in our DNA where the enemy can trigger it.

[7] See Realms of the Kingdom Volume 2 Chapter 3 – Familiar Spirits

[8] See Realms of the Kingdom Volume 1: Chapter 11 – Courtroom of God

Why do you think people who are involved in major church movements get involved in sin? Because the enemy says, "I am looking for a trigger in the autosome. Where has that thing been traded all the way down the family line? We demons own this piece here, so we will trigger it there." And so it triggers, and people behave in that way on the face of the earth. It is sin and it needs to be judged.

So you have got to judge *your* house. You must judge *this* house here first (yourself). The high priest would come into the realm of the presence of YHVH. I understand he would do various things and then he would take the scroll of the Word of God and raising it above his head he would say, "This has now become my covering. I stand under the covering of the dispensation of the Torah as a *huppah*." This is the realm that he had access to because he was a high priest for the children of Israel. So he stood as the mediator and to stand as the mediator he came under that covering.

The only covering I want in the new covenant is the covering of the Word of God on my head – Yeshua is my covering. I stand in the dispensation of the grace of my Messiah. Unless you experience the covering of His *huppah*, His Word, you will look for an earthly covering. And then whatever is going on in the earthly covering sits over you, and you trade into what *it* is doing!

The high priest would take responsibility: "I have sinned. This is *my* sin. This is my problem. These are my issues. I take full responsibility for it under this covering." Without this covering there is no life. The only way they could have life was to be under the covering of the Word. The high priest would say, "Judge me, oh YHVH, according to the measure of Your grace in the judgement of sin over me. Mediate the breaking of the condition of my people, of Your people, away from the condition of sin that sits in them." Then he would say, "Everywhere there has been iniquity, judge me, oh YHVH." *"Let your ear now be attentive, and your eyes open, that you may hear the prayer of your servant, which I pray before you now, day and night, for the children of Israel your servants, and confess the sins of the children of*

Israel, which we have sinned against you: both I and my father's house have sinned" (Nehemiah 1:6).

Iniquity

Iniquity is a bent towards something. It means you are a doer of your own thing. Yeshua said, "Many will say to me in that day, Lord, Lord, have we not prophesied in your name? And in your name have cast out demons? And in your name done many wonderful works? And then will I profess unto them, I never knew you: depart from me, you that work iniquity" (one who does your own thing).

"Many will say to me in that day, Lord, Lord, have we not prophesied in your name? and in your name have cast out demons? and in your name done many wonderful works? And then will I profess unto them, I never knew you: depart from me, you that work iniquity" (Matthew 7:22-23).

Do not do something just because it looks spiritual. Even if you have had 90,000 visions or 400 encounters with YHVH, my real question is, are you administrating that on the earth? If not, it is just a spiritual experience. Has it brought you to maturity? If it has not, it is a worthless spiritual experience. Just because you have had visions and have knowledge does not mean to say you are mature. Maturity is about responsibility in heaven. If you do not have responsibility in heaven, you are immature.

It is not even about being given a title like 'apostle'. I do not know whether you have noticed, but everyone who was a pastor in the 1960s suddenly became a teacher in the 1970s, then a prophet in the 1980s and an apostle in the 1990s. Within the title 'apostle' is *a mountain of influence and authority over that group.* Whoever is on top of the mountain is '*Who's Who in the Zoo*!' We all want to know *Who's Who in the Zoo*, so we all look in that zoo and wonder, "*Who's Who*?" That is what really happens.

In Africa they really struggle with me because I do not have a title before or after my name. I am not *Apostle* Ian. I am not *Prophet* Ian. I am not *Teacher* Ian. I am not *Pastor* Ian. I am not even ordained. But people say to me, "We need to have a title for you." And I say to them, "Then call me *'son'*." The only reason that there is an apostle, a prophet, a teacher, an evangelist and a pastor is to bring the body to maturity. Then when the body reaches maturity, this five-fold office is done away with. *"So Christ himself gave the apostles, the prophets, the evangelists, the pastors and teachers, to equip his people for works of service, so that the body of Christ may be built up until we all reach unity in the faith and in the knowledge of the Son of God and become mature, attaining to the whole measure of the fullness of Christ"* (Ephesians 4:11-13).

Transgression

Transgression is where you have knowingly, willingly, through an act of your *choice,* broken a law. Sinning is what you *do* when you break the law. There is a difference between sin and sinning. Sinning is the *action* that is associated with the bents inside you where you have broken the law and we need to take responsibility for those.

I believe we fully have Jesus as the Mediator of our confession, or the High Priest of our confession by coming under the government of the *huppah* of His covering, which means surrender to Lordship. There is a difference between fire-insurance (salvation) and the Lordship of Christ (assurance). You only have insurance if you have Him as Savior. But it is assurance of sonship if you have Him as Lord. I want Him as Lord so I bring myself under the covering of His Lordship: the domain of His *huppah* that sits over me.

The high priest would then say, "I have sinned: judge *me* oh YHVH according to Your covering." (Nehemiah 1:6-11, 9:27, Psalm 26:2, Psalm 43:1).

The Bible says, 'Judge my house', *"Thus says the LORD of hosts; If you will walk in my ways, and if you will keep my charge, then you shall also judge my house, and shall also keep my courts, and I will give you places to walk among these that stand here"* (Zechariah 3:7), which is different from the instruction, *"Do not judge and criticize and condemn others unfairly with an attitude of self-righteous superiority..."* (Matthew 7:1 AMP).

The best way to judge is to *be* judged first. So he would

say: "Judge *me*, oh YHVH, according to the measure of the covering that I am now under. And judge everything that is *outside* of this covering with the same measure that You judge me with *through* the covering of Yeshua ..."

Have you heard of a Flaming Sword? The Bible describes cherubim and a flaming sword in *the way* of the tree of life, not *'in front'* of the tree of life. "*... he placed at the east of the garden of Eden Cherubim, and a flaming sword which turned every way,* ***to guard the way*** *of the tree of life* (Genesis 3:24). *'The way'* is a pathway that leads to eternal life. Unless you bear the name you will never get on that pathway and you will never bear a name in heaven. YHVH has already given us a new name so we have got to bear that name which is our entry into the realm of heaven. If you do not have your new name, you have no entry.

The Bible says, "*And the angels who kept not their first estate, but left their own habitation*", (Jude 1:6). Their first estate is the name of the covering of their entry into heaven. At the tower of Babel they said, "*Come let us build ourselves a city, with a tower that reaches to the heavens, so that we may make a name for ourselves*" (Genesis 11:4). They said that because that name is their entry back into the realm of eternity. They wanted to live in their sin nature for eternity. God did not think so!

The high priest would stand and say, "Judge me, Oh YHVH, and then judge everything on the *outside* of this covering." And in that exact instant, the whole of the Israelite nation was free from every form of sin, iniquity and transgression. And grace was given for a whole year until the high priest would come in and do it again. "*...The priests always went into the first part of the tabernacle, performing the services. But into the second part the high priest went alone once a year, not without blood, which he offered for himself and for the people's sins committed in ignorance*" (Hebrews 9:6-7 NKJV).

The Bible says we have something better than the Old Testament. "*He is the mediator of a better covenant, which was established upon better promises*" (Hebrews 8:6). You can go into the YHVH's presence any time you like. You do not even have to get prepared to go in there. When you go in there Yeshua says, "Oh, I remember you. All that I have belongs to you, therefore you are totally righteous." Whatever you have been struggling with, the moment you enter the world of the Father, in the domain of His government, you are made totally righteous, because that is the only way you can stand there. Righteousness is a gift, *"For if by one man's offense death reigned by one; much more they who receive abundance of grace and of the gift of righteousness shall reign in life by one, Jesus Christ"* (Romans 5:17).

You cannot stand down here and say, "Give me the gift of righteousness." You have to go where it is. When you go where it is you receive it instantaneously. Every record of whatever you have been involved with and done is totally removed from you in heaven. It is done. But then we have to take responsibility for this thing left on the earth, which is your body.

As it is in heaven, so it is on the earth (Matthew 6:10). So if I want 'as it is in heaven' then I have to engage the heavenly realm and go where He is, to actually get righteousness. When I receive it, the Bible describes, *"The blessedness of the man, to whom God* ***imputes*** *righteousness without works"* (Romans 4:6). The word 'imputes' means to 'put in, or to be reckoned or attributed to a person'.

Yeshua *puts* righteousness into you when you go there. So the reality of our stepping in as a priest of the Lord is that, when I step in there, I become totally and absolutely righteous.

In Zechariah 3, Joshua the high priest comes before the Lord, and Satan stands beside him to resist him. Then God instructs his filthy garments to be removed. *"And he showed me Joshua the high priest standing before the angel of the LORD, and Satan standing at his right hand to accuse him. .... Now Joshua was clothed with filthy garments, and stood before the angel. And he answered and spoke unto those that stood before him, saying, Take away the filthy garments from him. And unto him he said, Behold, I have caused your iniquity to pass from you, and I will clothe you with rich apparel" (Zechariah 3:1-4).*

This means: no more sin, no more transgression, no more iniquity, and no more record of wrongdoing. "Excuse me devil, what are you doing here? Ah, you have come for judgment, Flaming Sword treatment (Genesis 3:24), to make you glow like glass. It will bend you and twist you until you are just a little mangled mess."

Warfare as many of us have been taught is: "I bind you in the name of Jesus." Well, instead of that, just go and actually allow YHVH to do what He wants to do. But when we do not go there, we do our own warring on the earth, because we have been told we have to do that. We are often taught to turn into darkness and focus on 'the enemy', but whatever you turn into becomes your supply. So the more you turn into darkness the greater the supply of darkness around your life, because you are drawing into that kingdom all the time. We do it because we have been told we have to.

Our role is to come into the world of our Father, and open up that world so the Kingdom of God can move. It becomes important for YHVH to engage us in those arenas because the facilitation of all that is important around our lives. We have got to go where He is so we can engage the truth of it here on the earth. Then we need to move in the presence of the Lord to open up that realm for us. But we have got to go there. That is why we are called 'priests of God'.

In the New Testament we are called priests and kings, (Revelation 5:10). But, before you can rule as a king, you have got to walk as a priest so your job is to go there and get clean by allowing judgement to come, under the dispensation of grace in Christ. "*...From Jesus the Messiah the witness, the faithful one the firstborn from the dead, and the ruler over the kings of the earth. To the one who loves us and has freed*[c] *us from our sins by his blood and has made us a kingdom, priests for his God and Father, be glory and power forever*" (Revelation 1:5-6 ISV).

In fact, you have got to *ask* for it because, remember, when you are here (in heaven) there is no record of this (what is on earth). In timelessness there is no record of time and what is held in time – zero record. So there is nothing the enemy can accuse you of there (in heaven).

But I want to have my body changed by what I do there (in heaven). So if the record of sin is in my body, and my spirit man lives in my body, and I want my spirit man to live on the outside of my body, the only way to get my spirit man on the outside is to deal with the body so that the body can become hosted by your spirit once again; instead of your body hosting your spirit.

Jesus knew all of this. He was in the temple when the high priest asked him "Are you the son of God?"

"Again the high priest asked him, and said to him, Are you the Christ, the Son of the Blessed? And Jesus said, I am…" (Mark 14:61-2).

When Yeshua spoke "I *Am*", He spoke the seventy Names of YHVH, which are the first syllable of every name from Adam all the way through to Yeshua. It is a story of the whole of salvation, in Name, frequency and vibration.

The priest got really mad with Him because He used the Name of YHVH, which is only supposed to be spoken in the Holy of Holies, out into the marketplace. It was not simply "I am". The Jews will not write the full Name of YHVH down. No rabbi will tell you the Name of YHVH. You have got to go on your own journey. I spent four years finding it out. So, Jesus spoke the Name of YHVH in the marketplace and the priests tore their cloaks. They picked up stones to stone Yeshua and He hid Himself in the temple (John 8:59). Greek thinking is like this: "I run away and I hide behind a pillar so they cannot see me." But the answer is found in the next verse which says He passed right through them and they did not see Him.

"*Then took they up stones to cast at him: but Jesus hid himself, and went out of the temple, going through the midst of them, and so passed by*"(John 8:59).

So, what temple did He hide himself in? I believe it was the temple of His spirit man because His spirit was able to host His body and hide it from this world. This transitions Him into another dimensional world that is right next to us that we have access to all the time. That is where you get totally clean and voluntarily bring yourself under judgment to judge yourself before the Lord. When you do that judgment, the record is then removed from the earth. This means there are no more triggers for the enemy to use people on the platform of the earth to form his own shadow to cause mischief.

But we have not learnt what it is to go in yet, because we are told: "Only one day, when we die, are we going to go there. Someday, in the ethereal world; and the Kingdom world is way out there. One day, when you die, it is all going to be made open and you will understand everything." Well actually, you will not understand everything when you die. You will only understand what you participated in here. That is going to be the measure of your maturity there. That is where your starting point is going to be. Then you have still got to be brought to maturity. "...*We speak wisdom among them that are mature: yet not the wisdom of this world, nor of the princes of this world, that come to nothing: But we speak the wisdom of God in a mystery, even the hidden wisdom, which God ordained before the world unto our glory*" (1 Corinthians 2:6-7). Your *inheritance* is going to be based on what you have done here. Have you fulfilled the scroll of your testimony or have you been busy doing your own thing that just looked good because people would recognise it as being spiritual? That is why Paul says: *"I have fought a good fight, I have finished my course, I have kept the faith: Henceforth there is laid up for me a crown of righteousness..."* (2 Timothy 4:7-8). 'Up there is laid up a crown because I have run my race, I have fulfilled my call.' He is talking about his scroll of testimony that came out of heaven with him. The scroll that he agreed with in the Y'sod[9] of YHVH, before he was on the earth when he was in the realm of eternity with his Father. He is saying he had a purpose to come to earth to fulfil because he wanted a higher inheritance than he had before. So he came down to the earth and fulfilled that scroll.

When it is finished, that book is going to speak of itself. It will bear witness in heaven as to what you have done. The book of your works is going to be opened up in that day and your reward is going to be according to your works (Revelation 20:12). Your reward will not be according to anything you decided to do but according to how much of your testimony scroll you birthed onto the earth, and that relates to the role

[9] The Y'Sod is one of the heavenly courts. More information can be found at: www.sonofthunder.org

that you played in heaven before you were in the earth. *"For we are his workmanship, created in Christ Jesus unto good works, which God has before ordained that we should walk in them"* (Ephesians 2:10). I do a further teaching on this called 'Where do I Come From'. You have got to understand where you have come from to understand where you are going back to. Hebrew people think in a circular way: 1+2+3 = 6 = +3+2+1. The end must always equal the beginning.

The high priest would judge himself. So we need to ask the Sword of God, the Flaming Sword of YHVH which is in the way of the tree of life, to come and judge us according to the testimony of the two cherubim (Genesis 3:24). Why are there two cherubim? Well, we presently have a two-stranded cord of DNA. Without the Sword of the light of YHVH 's judgment, that DNA will never be able to enter into the fullness of the knowledge of YHVH. So judgment becomes important. You have got to judge your own house.

I have taught practical sessions elsewhere about how to 'step in' by faith. In the atmosphere of the Kingdom, the realm of YHVH is accessible, and it is actually right there. This is how close it is: Yeshua is praying for a blind man. He takes His spit and puts it on the ground, mixes it, puts it on the man's eyes and his eyes open, *"And he looked up, and said, I see men as trees, walking. Once more Jesus put his hands on the man's eyes. Then his eyes were opened, his sight was restored, and he saw everything clearly."* (Mark 8:24-25). When the man saw men as trees, Yeshua was saying, 'Oh, sorry, wrong realm, you should see into this one.' The realm of heaven is as close to you as the air that you breathe. What he was seeing when he saw men as tall as trees walking was the sons of YHVH from the first creation. There are two creations: The first creation when YHVH made sons and the second creation when He made Adam. Further teaching on these subjects can be downloaded from my website: www.sonofthunder.org

By faith, we need to be able to step through into the world of the Father, into the realm of His Kingdom, into the realm of His presence, which is as close to us as the air that we breathe. By faith, I can step through that veil which Yeshua tore open, and I can stand there. The moment I enter that world, it is recorded that I have become absolutely and totally righteous before the presence of YHVH. Because, if there is any record over me, YHVH declares, "That cannot come here, get it off him, and put a new garment on him. In fact, put a crown upon his head, and then, actually, put a ring on his finger." (Zechariah 3:4-5) And then you and I can stand before Him.

Practise by placing a Bible on your head and saying, "By faith, Lord, I stand under the government of Your Word. I stand under the Lordship of Christ *as my covering,* because You are the High Priest of my confession. Jesus, I ask that You would take Your Word like a sword, that Flaming Sword that stands in the way of the tree of life and I ask that You would judge me according to the dispensation of grace, (which is why the throne of grace is there). And according to the dispensation of grace, judge me according to the confession of my sin."

Here, at this point, I would say: "This is what I have done… *da-da-da*… I ask You to remove that from my life. Judge it according to Your testimony which is 'righteousness in Christ Jesus'. Remove it from my life." (See also 'Court Room of God' in Realms of the Kingdom Volume 1).

Now, Lord, as You have judged me, I ask You to judge everything that was connected to that part of my life with the same sword that I have asked You to go through *my* life with.

Standing under the Lordship of Christ provides covering. Everything outside it gets burned up to a crisp, burnt to ash (1 Corinthians 3:15). Demonic things have a right of access to the record that is connected to your life on the earth. So when you stand in heaven and you bring that record, as a spirit-being, into heaven and you ask YHVH to judge it, the (demonic) record on earth begins to get burnt to a crisp in that area and the devil cries, "Oh no! They are finally doing what YHVH wants them to do, and we have kept it hidden from them for so long. They have never done this before. Now we are going to get beaten up because this Flaming Sword is coming after us!"

When I was in a particular nation, I talked in a church on this subject, about the judgment. When this truth landed, riots opened up because of the demonic stuff that was going on. I felt responsible for what happened there. It went on for two days. So I went into the church and I said, "Okay, I am going to teach you about judgment because I want *us* to take responsibility for this sin. We are going to judge it today. I am going to teach you how to judge something in a nation."

So we took all those present into the court. The whole church went in, about a hundred and eighty people. We took that thing into court and said: "*I* have sinned. This is *my* sin. According to this testimony judge *me* Lord. Now, Lord, any demon that is connected to this we ask you to judge them." Within an hour all the riots had finished.

We have administrative roles in heaven on the earth. But you have got to be in heaven to facilitate that role on the earth. You have a role to play. That role is not difficult, but you have got to judge yourself and take responsibility for sin.

I have been on a journey, walking through the autosomes of my DNA, dealing with every record and I have found stuff in my DNA from previous overshadowings. Let me tell you, when you deal with your issues, things change. That is because the record down here, which is called your human body, begins to vibrate at a different frequency because it is now bearing a different shadow of 'as it is in heaven.'

There will come a point where our bodies are going to take on the resurrection glory of that realm and that will be opened up for us down here. When that opens up, you and I are going to have a body that shines like Yeshua's did when He was transfigured. We all think that one day, when we die, we are going to go into heaven, and God is going to say, "*This is my beloved Son, in whom I am well pleased*" (Matthew 3:17). But when the Father spoke to Jesus like that, He was alive and living on the earth. Do you think it cannot happen to us if it happened to Christ? When He showed us the way and how to do it?

Yeshua made a way for the fullness of YHVH to be revealed in us in Christ Jesus. Everything can be revealed in us through the nature of what He has presented to us. Everything Yeshua ever did was recorded for us, to show us the Way. As Jesus is the Way, the Truth and the Life (John 14:6), you have got to be cloaked or 'skinned' with the three skins of the Father: judgment, justice and holiness (Isaiah 5:16); the three skins of the Holy Spirit: righteousness, joy and peace (Romans 14:17); and the three skins of Yeshua: the way the truth and the life (John 14:6). This all links into the building of a frequency platform for the testimony of heaven to rest and manifest on the earth.

I believe in practice, so we must practise judging ourselves under the dispensation of grace in Christ Jesus. You have got to judge the house of the Lord as we see in Zechariah 3:7. You will judge *your* house, *this* house here (yourself), because *this* house is going to bear the record of the testimony of heaven. It has to, in order for us to terraform and change the earth back into what it was before sin. If we are to make the whole earth like a well-watered garden (Isaiah 35, 58:11), then we need to change *this* (ourselves), because then *this* will be able to judge *that*.

I want you to see the responsibility here. The whole of creation, every dimensional world, the whole of our universe, every single thing that is organic, every single thing that is spiritual in that whole arena is looking at you on the earth. It is all saying, "Get your act together. Our galaxy has hundreds of billions of stars in it all looking at you saying, "Get your act together!" Our little solar system is saying, "Get your act together!" The whole of our universe is saying, "Get your act together!" Every other dimensional world outside of our universe is saying, "Get your act together!" We need you to take your place so that we have admission to a kingly government once again, so that there is no more darkness. We do not like being in darkness!" We would be very naive to think that in a possible two trillion galaxies (found to date); there are no other beings made that understand this truth. But we are the only ones that hold the potential record to rule (Genesis 1:26, 28). That is why everything wants our DNA. The earth is the centre of the Father's creation.

Our Father is saying to us, "Do not worry about Sister Rub and Brother Sandpaper next to you. Do not worry about what they think about you in the church. Chase Me, and do what I am asking you to do. When you do what I have asked you to do and you have been conformed to My image, then all of creation will sing, '*Aaahh*! At long last!'" (Romans 8:19). So this is how it starts, this little thing of stepping in. It is so simple, it is not hard.

There are seven different arenas or domains of our Father: there is the kingdom of the earth, the Kingdom of God, the Kingdom of heaven, heaven, heaven of heavens, Perfection and Eternity. In the kingdom of the earth, which is the lowest arena and domain of our Father, we have access to His world and the domain of His presence in the kingdom of the earth. So when we step through the veil we are stepping into the realm of His presence in the kingdom of the earth. We do not have to go *all* the way up there yet. Maturity will get you there. You have got to start with this first.

Practice Court Session

I would like you to take something that you can put over your head such as the Bible, your cell phone, a little bit of paper or anything. It is just a symbol because I believe in body-participation. That means body, soul, and spirit are all in agreement with what we are doing.

Yeshua tore that veil to give me entry into His kingdom. Close your eyes and practise taking a small step forwards, then take a small step backwards.

In front of you is a veil that separates you from the realm of His presence. Yeshua tore that open. So, Father, today by faith, in the name of Yeshua, we step through that torn veil *(take a small step forward)*.

Lord, we step through the torn veil into the realm of Your presence. Father, I want to thank You that as I stand here today,

You remove from my life every stained record ever held in my DNA as I stand before You as a person.

Lord, You give me a garment of righteousness that I receive by faith because it is a gift from my Father to me, to empower me to be able to stand and become a priest of God in this realm of Your Kingdom.

Father, today I bring myself under the covering *(put something on your head),* the covering of the testimony of Christ as my High Priest, the Firstborn Son of many. I stand under His covering today, freely and willingly.

(Now, in your mind take an area of your life that you have struggled with and come into agreement with the following prayer.)

Father, today I bring You this part of my life that I have been wrestling with. I have been married and connected to it. I have allowed it expression in my body as a sound in my DNA. I have allowed it to be triggered by the enemy and used as a place of sacrifice and offering to his world and his kingdom. Father, I bring this area of my life into the light before You. Today, Jesus, I thank you that you are the High Priest of my confession. I confess this today as sin, iniquity and transgression that have separated me from the reality of 'in heaven on earth.'

Father, today I ask that You would take Your Flaming Sword, that Sword that stands in the way of the tree of life and under the covering of Your Lordship, and I ask You to judge the record in my physical body and judge the record in my soul where sin has held me bound to the testimony of this behaviour. Lord, as You judge me, I open my heart for judgment today.

Now, Lord, I ask You to judge anything that is on the *outside* of this covering and everything that was connected to that part of my life. I ask You to judge it today according to the dispensation of Your judgment over *me.* Father, today, judge this stain and blemish in the record of my DNA that has been triggered by the enemy. Judge it on earth as it is being judged in heaven today. Lord, remove the record of it.

Father, today by faith, I ask that in the scribal council[10] and the court of the scribes You would give me a divorce paper from this condition and this behavioural pattern in my life. I willingly ascribe and declare that I am divorced from this condition and its power over my life. In every place I have yielded to it, today I separate myself from it. I divorce myself from it according to the testimony of this written document in the courts of heaven. I willingly receive the divorce papers today.

Now Lord, by faith, I marry the presence of Christ in this area that the testimony of the light of Yeshua would so shine in this record in my body on earth that it would destroy every work of the enemy connected to this part of my life.

Father, by faith, I thank You for this garment that You have given me for the cleansing, purity and holiness that I have received in heaven here today.

Lord, by faith, I step back into my body, into the world of the earth, bringing with me the testimony of this judgment into my body. Lord, I administrate it into the record of my DNA, into the record of my life, and the book of my life.

I ask You to administrate that justice and judgment into my body today as a witness so that it is on earth as it is in heaven, in Yeshua's mighty name. Hallelujah, Lord! Amen.

When I do this, I feel so good, but here is the issue: you have got to practise. Practice makes perfect. Once you know the way you can become perfect in the way and then you become perfect as He is perfect. As Jesus said, *"Be you therefore perfect, even as your Father who is in heaven is perfect"* (Matthew 5:48) The reason Paul could say that he was perfect, was because he knew about some of this.

We need to practise every day. I practice this all the time. I have walked this thing out for many years. Now it takes me less than thirty seconds to do. When I find myself responding to something that is inordinate, I just go in, open up, stand there, judge it, get divorce papers and then I step back onto the earth. It is done on earth as it is in heaven.

[10] This is one of the councils of YHVH, more information is available at: www.sonofthunder.org

But I bring it *out* of heaven *to* the earth. You cannot stand down here asking God to do it. You have got to go where He is, because the only realm where you can get changed is the heavenly realm. You cannot change this world without being changed there first.

Chapter 6
Our Priestly Role

"Therefore if any man be in Christ, he is a new creation: old things are passed away; behold, all things are become new" (2 Corinthians 5:17).

For those whom He foreknew He also predestined to be conformed to the image of His Son, so that He might be the firstborn among many brothers and sisters (Romans 8:29 TLV).

Our priestly role within the Order of Melchizedek means the human genetics passed down from our family line is forsaken and completely changed. We are transformed, conformed and engaged with the genetics and the genealogy we inherited in Christ when we were born again. "For in him we live, and move, and have our being" (Acts 17:28).

Terminate sin at the beginning

Our capacity as a priest is to go back to the beginning, where the beginning and the end meet and be able to administrate from that position, so we can terminate sin at its conception. We go into the Lamb, slain before the foundation of the world, where we become a 'complete being'. Then bringing that completeness into our day we frame our world out of that completeness. As we do this we will be able to frame it from the source of the beginning when there was no record of sin.

From this place, we will frame life, because where the

beginning is, also is the end of a matter. From this position, we will see the end of the matter as well as the beginning of the matter at the same time. We will be able to live within the realm of the beginning and the end, and will understand the fullness of any decision that is made, because there, we will also see the end of it. This will empower us to walk righteously because we will be able to see the beginning and end of every decision we make at the same time.

That is one of the ways we walk in the Spirit, and that is how we will also be led by the Spirit. *"Walk in the Spirit, and you shall not fulfill the lust of the flesh"* (Galatians 5:16), because you see the end of every decision. So you only make right decisions. There is a circle: the end meets beginning.

Administrate 'Holy' onto the earth to reframe the world

Part of the role of Melchizedek is to administrate holiness that YHVH reveals, *"And the four living creatures had each of them six wings about him; and they were full of eyes within: and they rest not day and night, saying, Holy, holy, holy, Lord God Almighty, who was, and is, and is to come"* (Revelation 4:8). 'Holy' means "Wow! Did you see that? Awesome!" It is something indescribable in human terms.

Part of what happens here is that our role as a Melchizedek priest is to administrate the revelation of the glory of the Lord into the land of the living by actually standing as a priest and gazing into the Glory of YHVH. I have taught on the cherubim standing on either side of the mercy seat and what they do when they look in (See Realms of the Kingdom Volume 2, Understanding Angels) and continually cry Holy, Holy, Holy! Our administration as a priest is to do the same as they have done and administrate "Holy": "The (cherubim) facing into the glory are crying,"Holy is the Lord" (Isaiah 6:2, Revelation 4:8). Opening their wings they display the reflection of their observance, turning and administrating 'holy' into all of creation saying, "They are holy as He is holy", then looking at one another saying, "you are holy as He is Holy". By using their pattern and the decree of your mouth, as a priest from that world and place, you will be able to frame the world of revelation by what you are seeing around the throne of YHVH. Then you bring that as a priest into your day and you frame the world out of your own revelation of 'holy'. Our job as a priest is to administrate 'holy' around the throne of YHVH and then to be able to engage with that here in this world.

'Holy' is not simply a religious word we speak. It means: "Wow! Did you see that!" It means revelation! Revelation is what Satan traded on in Ezekiel 28: *"By your great wisdom and by your trade have you increased your riches, and your heart is lifted up because of your riches...by the multitude of your trade they have filled the midst of you with violence, and you have sinned"* (Ezekiel 28:5, 16). I believe that on the second day of creation, as a covering cherubim, Lucifer saw the revelation of what YHVH would do with man – because the second day is the only day YHVH did not say, "It was good" (Genesis1:6-8).

In the administration of 'holy' you frame the world (speak life and definition) out of the observance of revelation, not the revelation someone else teaches you. What someone else teaches you shows you a way to frame your world to get your own revelation.

"Man shall not live by bread alone, but by every Word that proceeds out of the mouth of God" (Matthew 4:4). You cannot see the Word proceeding unless you are standing with YHVH, watching Him speak. When YHVH speaks, His Word is framed into being. So when you actually bring that frame here, you can bring His Word to bear, to frame His world within this world.

The High Priest had the Urim and Thummim. They were two stones that I believe the high priest would put behind the breast plate of 12 stones when he had to judge something to find the truth, the stones would arc and light up. The high priest would then turn and face the veil and the light would shine through the breast plate stones in the language inscribed within those 12 stones. YHVH would then speak (like looking at a movie in language) through the 12 stones on the breast plate. This is why and how they knew if someone was talking truth by taking this and putting it inside their garment.

"The God of our Lord Jesus Christ, the Father of glory, may give unto you the spirit of wisdom and revelation" (Ephesians 1:17). YHVH is going to give the Melchizedek priesthood discernment like Aaron had with the Urim and Thummim, *"And you shall put in the breastplate of judgment the Urim and the Thummim; and they shall be upon Aaron's heart, when he goes in before the LORD: and Aaron shall bear the judgment of the children of Israel upon his heart before the LORD continually"* (Exodus 28:30). This is to give the ability to know the truth of everything that is proceeding before them and out of everyone that is around them so they can bring the truth to bear in right judgment because, when they know the truth, *"...the truth shall make you free"* (John 8:32). That is why Jesus knew things, because, *"...He knows about everyone, everywhere"* (Hebrews 4:13 TLB). All through the Bible it says, *"Jesus knew immediately what they were thinking"* (Mark 2:8 NLT), or *"Before Philip called you, when you were under the fig tree, I saw you"* (John 1:48). *"He knows about everyone, everywhere. Everything about us is bare and wide open to the all-seeing eyes of our living God; nothing can be hidden from him..."* (Hebrews 4:13 TLB). *"He that has an ear, let him hear what the Spirit says unto the churches; To him that overcomes will I give to eat of the hidden manna, and will give him a white stone, and in the stone a new name written, which no man knows except him who receives it"* (Revelation 2:17).

"He has covered me with the robe of righteousness" (Isaiah 61:10). the truth is going to be seen wherever we go, like having spiritual urim and thummin on our priestly robes. The truth will expose every single lie, including the triggers that sit inside our life from our genealogy line. It will expose the full truth of what is going on.

This is why the world will try to destroy you because they will not like the truth coming out. Within that truth we will function and be able to judge because we will have learned what it is to judge in righteousness, through being judged by righteousness and understanding the process and protocol of judgment because we have learned about being judged. See the chapter *'Judge My House'* and Realms of the Kingdom Volume 1, *Courtroom of God.*

The issue of the truth being found and framed will become very important for us. We will be able to frame truth and bring truth into every area including government. I cannot wait to actually function in this way. Can you imagine when we can stand in front of someone and say, "Well actually, that is a lie, here is the truth of heaven. This is what it looks like – have a look."

"Jesus saw Nathanael coming to him, and said of him, Behold an Israelite indeed, in whom is no guile! Nathanael said unto him, Where do you know me? Jesus answered and said unto him, Before Philip called you, when you were under the fig tree, I saw you" (John 1:47-48). If you are a priest, you should be able to take others with you to the very end and the very beginning. You should be able to let them see the beginning from the end, and let them understand that the decisions they are making are going to bring fruit. We will show them that, if they only want fruits of righteousness, then this is what they need to be doing. *"But we have the mind of Christ"* (1 Corinthians 2:16). You will become a television screen for revelation to lead nations. That is why *"Nations will come to your light, And kings to the brightness of your rising"* (Isaiah 60:3 AMP). Nations will come to the light of your shining because the gate of eternity will be now fully open in your heart. *"Lift up your heads, O you gates; and be you lifted up, you everlasting doors; and the King of glory shall come in"* (Psalm 24:7).

Years ago I learned how to scrap in the right way with the demonic world because of understanding judgment. He would come as the accuser and say, "You are a sinner! *Rar-rar-rar*!" I would say, "Yes, I am." He would then say, "Uhh! You are not supposed to say that, you are supposed to say, 'No, I am not!' and fight me." And I would say, "Oh, let us have a look." I would open up the spiritual cavity of my chest and show him my heart because in there is the realm of eternity, there is no record of the demonic in this realm and neither is there a record of your sin.

When the gate of your heart is opened under the Order of the Melchizedek priesthood, you cannot continually commit sin (1 John 3:9). Not because you do not want to but because there is no record for its power within you, because you already know the end from the beginning and your choices are all formed around the glory of the knowledge of YHVH. *"For the earth shall be filled with the knowledge of the glory of the LORD, as the waters cover the sea"* (Habakkuk 2:14).

Reconcile nations back to the very beginning

Part of the process under the Order of Melchizedek is operating as an oracle, through this we will be able to reconcile nations back to their true testimony, as they were originally purposed in the foundation that YHVH created for each when He established them, as they were formed. Helping the body of Christ walk in the truth of the testimony written on each scroll, for nations as well as individuals. The truth of the scroll of that nation's testimony will be unrolled for us to speak as oracles of YHVH from the Council of God (Psalm 82:1), the Sanhedrin of heaven. We will be able to come as an emissary with papers from the Sanhedrin to bring justice onto the earth to bring each nation back to the full knowledge of what it was designed to be.

Mediator of the eternal world into the earth

"I sought for a man among them, that should build up the wall, and stand in the gap before me for the land, that I should not destroy it" (Ezekiel 22:30). As a priest in the Order of Melchizedek, we will become a mediator of the eternal world into this world, so we will be able to bring into this world the eternal world. From that eternal world, we will be able to precipitate everything that is needed so that YHVH can frame this world by the mediation of our confession. "As it is written, I have made you a father of many nations,) before him whom he believed, even God, who gives life to the dead, and calls those things which are not as though they were" (Romans 4:17). From the mediation of our confession, we will be able to bring the reality of heaven into earth, bringing into earth that world so that this world can be changed back into the form of its original design.

This world originally came out of that YHVH's world. When the earth was first formed, it was formed from the substance of the eternal world. Out of the eternal creative light of YHVH it came into existence when He spoke it into being. Due to what happened with Adam YHVH confined the nature and the record of sin in time and space. When time and space is done away with there will be no more record of sin and the world will be able to take its original place in the will of the Father.

Power and life flows and functions from the center outwards, not from the outside in. Remember, in YHVH's original design there was Eden, and YHVH planted a garden eastward in Eden. *"And a river went out of Eden to water the garden; and from there it was parted, and became four heads"* (Genesis 2:10) and watered the earth.

The Bible names four rivers (Genesis 2:11-14). Today, these actually are the four chambers of your heart because the river flows through you now, not out of the spirit world. Your heart is supposed to take the world back to the way it was originally formed. Adam was supposed to take this record and grow it in the earth. This is why your heart is so important as a priest and oracle because out of it flows the issues of life (Proverbs 4:23).

When sin entered, YHVH cut off the flow from Eden onto the earth. These 4 rivers at their entry point into creation upon the earth I believe are now known as everlasting doors that are laid down and not open (Psalm 24:7). They are controlled by *"...spiritual wickedness in heavenly places"* (Ephesians 6:12). And all that sit underneath them are shrouded with darkness. Yeshua was shown the kingdoms of this world, not the kingdoms of the earth.

I personally believe that the earth was originally at the center of YHVH's design. When sin entered, YHVH shifted the earth and put it within time and space, so it now revolves around the outside instead of being in the centre. YHVH is going to shift us back into the middle again. In Christ we are going to be able to mediate the eternal world into the earth to take the earth back into its eternal design thus creating a new heaven and a new earth.

OUR PRIESTLY CLOTHES

1) Golden girdle

The high priests wore a golden belt, or a girdle, that went around their waist. That girdle is also talked about in the book of Revelation. *"I (John) turned... to see... One like the Son of man, clothed with a garment down to the feet and girded about the chest with a golden band. His head and hair were white, like wool, as white as snow and His eyes like a flame of fire. His feet were like fine brass, as if refined in a furnace, and His voice as the sound of many waters... out of His mouth went a sharp two-edged sword, and His countenance was like the sun shining in its strength"* (Rev 1:12-15 NKJV)

That is what you look like when you stand in the spirit – not like the little mirror-image that you see each day. That is why the devil hates you to be in the spirit because he knows when you are in there, you look different than you do when you stand in the earth trying to be spiritual.

The golden girdle we wear is an investment of YHVH in our priestly mantle, so we are able to mediate the fullness of the government of YHVH into the earth. As the sons of YHVH stand in maturity, true government starts to flow, things that have never been seen will begin to happen.

2) Breastplate

The high priests also wore a breastplate. Every single part of the priestly garment represents an operation of something we are supposed to be functioning under within the Order of Melchizedek as a priest.

As mentioned earlier, twelve stones are on the breastplate (Exodus 28:21). We wear them on our breastplate as a symbol of an external-internal condition where we are fully immersed into the life of the nature of the person of our Father. Our job is to come before the Lord. And then out of those twelve stones reflect that revelation, the same way as the cherubim, that were only covered in nine stones (Ezekiel 28:13-14). They would say 'Holy' looking at 'Holy' with the revelation percolating. They would open their wings and shout *"Holy!"* When they would shout *"Holy"* and were in the position of revealing the glory to creation saying, "You are Holy as He is Holy!" When they would did that, the revelation coming from that realm would hit the nine stones and be reflected out into the universe. Then, they would close their wings around and look at one another and shout *"Holy!"* What they were saying is, "You are Holy as He is Holy!" The reason they could do this, is because they had been made Holy by what they had seen in the revelation. You and I are like them when we gazed upon that same place as a priest. It has so changed you that you take on the complete image of that revelation by your observance and position. That is why, when we see Him, we will get changed into His image, *"Beloved, now are we the children of God, and it does not yet appear what we shall be: but we know that, when he shall appear, we shall be like him; for we shall see him as he is"* (1 John 3:2), the key is not just to hear a voice but to actually see Him. The breastplate is a major piece of the priestly clothing that sits on our body. There is much more to say about this but it is planned for a future book.

3) White garment

We wear a white garment. *"I put on righteousness, and it clothed me. My justice was like a robe and a turban!"* (Job 29:14 AMP). *"But you [still] have a few people in Sardis who have not soiled their clothes [that is, contaminated their character and personal integrity with sin]; and they will walk with Me [dressed] in white, because they are worthy (righteous)"* (Revelation 3:4 AMP).

There were a number of layers of garments that the priests wore. There was a very fine linen garment that the priest used to wear underneath his external garment. The external garment was changed from priest to priest and I believe each one was taken and sewn onto the inside of the veil, so that the next priest would come through the relationship and encounter of those that went before him, to make it easier for him to come into the presence of YHVH. In a similar way, Jesus is the Door and going through Him makes it easier for us to have an encounter with YHVH.

That fine linen garment is actually what we are going to be

clothed with under the Order of Melchizedek. We will not need this body anymore because our body will be clothed in pure white light, *"His face did shine as the sun, and his clothing was white as the light"* (Matthew 17:2). And it is going to look like lightening. You are not going to have to move with your feet. The lightening will move you because you will be the ultimate power source!

4) Priestly Mantle of Christ

Yeshua made a really interesting statement. He said to his disciples in John 6:62: *"What if you shall see the Son of man ascend up to where he was before?"* And it says that some really got offended. In John 6:66, which is the number of the mark of the Beast (Revelation 13:17-18), the Word says: *"From that time many of His disciples went back and walked no more with Him"* (John 6:66). Part of the process of what Yeshua said then was important because the Hebrew people knew what happened with Elijah and Elisha. When Elijah was taken up in the whirlwind of fire he was not taken up in a chariot like we are taught, he was taken up in a whirlwind. The chariot came and the fiery horses came to separate that which must go into heaven from that which must remain on the earth (or else Elisha would have been taken up as well). *"… suddenly a chariot of fire appeared with horses of fire, and separated the two of them; and Elijah went up in a whirlwind into heaven."* (2 Kings 2:11).

They knew the history so, when Jesus said, *"what will you say if you see the Son of man ascend up to where he was before"* (John 6:62), what He was really saying is, "Hey, this is going to happen, the same thing as happened with Elijah and Elisha. I am going to be separated from you and what comes off My life is going to come on yours!"

So, when you see Him, you have what has come off His life, because the mantle that sat on Him will rest on you and as He moves your heart you will become a priest, *"A new heart also will I give you, and a new spirit will I put within you"* (Ezekiel 36:26).

Chapter 7
Kingship

Within the boundaries of the Order of Melchizedek, one of the faces is a king. YHVH calls us kings and priests of our God so we need to understand kingship (1 Peter 2:9, Revelation 1:6). A king is a judge, a provider and a protector. God gave Adam dominion over the earth to rule it and subdue it (Genesis 1:26, 28). That is the role of a king. Kingship means responsibility. When you are a king and sitting on your throne, your children cannot come up to you and say, "Daddy, daddy", and neither can the rest of the court. They have been taught about the reverence of the governmental seat that you are sitting on. There is power when you sit on that seat.

In the Order of Melchizedek, YHVH gives you a seat, or a throne, to sit on (Ephesians 2:6). From that throne you can execute judgment into the earth (1 Corinthians 2:15, John 7:24). Judgment is not always to bring death. We think judgment means someone will die but YHVH's judgment is often to bring a greater form of life. Even if there has to be some death, it is often to bring a greater form of life to pass.

A king has a vial of oil that will never run dry

The seat of a king is governmental but it is also supposed to provide for those that are connected to it. In the Order of Melchizedek, a king's seat has an inexhaustible supply to feed the poor, clothe the needy, and assist the widow. He has a vial of oil that will never run dry. It will feed the candlesticks of the needs of the nation. I have been talking to you about materializing matter. When you are in this full measure as a king, and you understand the pattern, you can create whatever is needed including gold. Gold is simply a chemical element with a specific density, atomic mass, number of protons, electrons and neutrons. Where do you think gold actually comes from? Was it formed on the earth or in heaven, and then released into the earth? The purest gold is seen in white quartz, because the purest gold is on the Sea of Crystal in heaven which used to flow into the earth because of the fountains of the deep. These were then sealed, so now they are white quartz which has seams of gold in them.

The king's seat is very important for us. When you sit on the seat, you will be able to change everything (Mark 9:23). There are some things YHVH gives to a king that He does not give to anyone else.

A king's sceptre and a staff

"Yea, though I walk through the valley of the shadow of death, I will fear no evil: for you are with me; your rod and your staff they comfort me" (Psalm 23:4). Understanding the function of the rod and the staff explains what the king is supposed to do when he sits on the throne. The rod (sceptre) is something that reaches before you to bring the government of YHVH into everything that stands in front of you. It makes a way for government to move through. The staff, which is the shepherd's crook, follows behind you, sometimes cleaning up the mess, which is part of the shepherding role as a King.

When the Bible talks about us walking through the valley of the shadow of death, it means that death is not going to have any power over us because there is an authority that sits in our life to execute justice against death. The shepherd's rod, is able to bring all those that follow Him into that realm of government out of death.

The shepherd's crook (or staff) was an amazing thing. It used to be made out of vines that were bent and then dried. It had a hoop or hook on it, often with another very small hook on the end of that. The tiny hook was useful when a sheep was naughty, and wandered into confined places or got lost in the mountains. The shepherd would literally leg-shackle it. That little hook would go into the inside leg of the sheep and the shepherd would pull on it. The sheep's leg would jam into the crook and then he could swing it over the cliff and onto the land. God has His shepherd's crook out for us and He brings us back into order. The Order of Melchizedek equips you with the ability to bring divine order into rebellion, to swing rebellion out of its condition and bring it into its rightful place which is in front of you. When a shepherd would swing the sheep around, he would face it. This means it comes under the rod. The rod brings divine order. The rod and the staff comfort us because they give us power in the day of darkness.

A king has power to bring creative light into black matter

Power is associated with the king's seat of government. I do not just mean power to heal the sick. I mean power to move stars and mountains. *"I assure you and most solemnly say to you, whoever says to this mountain, 'Be lifted up and thrown into the sea!' and does not doubt in his heart [in God's unlimited power], but believes that what he says is going to take place, it will be done for him [in accordance with God's will]"* (Mark 11:23 AMP). It would cause a bit of a stir if you stood in one part of your nation and said, "You, Mountain, over there". The government would be very interested in that. That is the kind of power that comes with the Order of Melchizedek when the king's seat is sat upon in the right way with maturity as its foundation. It enables you to terraform everything around you by bringing divine order. Power comes from the kingdom world. It does not come from the earthly world.

We are supposed to engage with governmental process. But YHVH wants to release understanding in us that with power comes great responsibility. As a king you will be called to pass judgments that may carry serious consequences. The king's seat is not necessarily a nice seat. You have to take responsibility for everything you do. And when you change one thing, it affects many other things because everything is inter-connected. There is something called *the butterfly effect* in quantum physics. A butterfly can do one thing over here and it can cause a tornado over there if the effect is right. This is quantum physics. Everything has a cause and effect.

When you sit on the seat of a king, then you have great power. You have power to form galaxies, power to re-form them, power to bring creative light back into black matter. The role of our kingship in Christ is to shine the light into darkness so everything in darkness can become light once again. The Order of Melchizedek, through the kingship, is going to bring light into every single particle in space presently called black matter and dark energy.

A king's wealth comes from the treasury room of heaven

Wealth also comes with being a king. People claim, "I am going to be like Joseph", but they have no idea about how the world's financial systems operate. The wealth that is coming is not coming from the work of your hands. It will come out of the treasury room of heaven. There is a lot of gold in that treasury room and Melchizedek is in charge of it all. I can witness to the role of Melchizedek as the Chief Chancellor of the Treasury Room of heaven. He handles all the riches of heaven. You need to know that, if you take the role and function within that priesthood's likeness, that treasury room is going to be open to you. This means you will be able to bring into the earth's atmosphere gold and provision out of that realm because provision and government are within the seat of a king. You will be able to materialize matter. You need some food? Here is food.

These are the things you have to start getting your brain around. You can walk into a desert and breathe out to form trees all around you. When you need water, you can speak to the earth and the earth will respond, open up and suddenly manifest a supply of water in front of you. *"And the LORD said unto Moses, Go on before the people, and take with you of the elders of Israel; and your rod, with which you smote the river, take in your hand, and go. Behold, I will stand before you there upon the rock in Horeb; and you shall strike the rock, and there shall come water out of it, that the people may drink. And Moses did so in the sight of the elders of Israel"* (Exodus 17:5-6).

This is our role as kings, bringing provision back into the world. This is power. This is what power is for. This is why the Order of Melchizedek is going to surpass the Kingdom Age because the Apostolic cannot do that. Its power is inside the church, not in creation. Great wealth is going to be generated because of who you are and what you can materialize.

Government will sit on your shoulders

The government is going to sit upon *your* shoulders. The Bible says that the government shall sit upon Jesus' shoulders. *"For unto us a child is born, unto us a son is given; and the government shall be upon his shoulder: and his name shall be called Wonderful, Counselor, The Mighty God, The everlasting Father, The Prince of Peace." (*Isaiah 9:6). If you are made like Him, you need to believe that you are going to be displayed like Him and that you are supposed to carry the same responsibility *"…Whoever believes in Me will be able to do what I have done, but they will do even greater things, because I will return to be with the Father"* (John 14:12 TLV). This is about government. As I have said before, if you were to say to your elected government in the land, "Today, it is going to rain continually. Except at my word, it will not stop raining" (1 Kings 17:1). They would laugh at first. But not, if two years later, it was still raining, and they had floods all over the nation with every river breaking its banks. If the seas started to encroach on the land because the level of the water had come up, they would come looking for you because they would know they were not in charge anymore. True government is going to be formed on the shoulders of the sons of YHVH within the order of Melchizedek. These are the things that I dream about.

We bring legislative paperwork from the Sanhedrin of heaven

YHVH is going to give to the king the ability to legislate from heaven to the earth. You need to study the word 'legislate'.

It means to make laws and decrees, pass laws and be able to pass legislation. Kingship is all about power because it is the roar of the Lion *"He'll roar like a lion, and when He roars, His children will scurry in from the west"* (Hosea 11:10 VOICE). When the Order of Melchizedek operates out of the face of kingship, it is going to operate out of the mouth of the Lion. It will roar and the earth will either scream in terror, or it will come to the light of your shining (Isaiah 60:3). We are going to shine. We really are going to shine. When we legislate out of heaven, you will find that the government of YHVH will back your words.

And so, when we legislate things, we are going to be able to bring effective change that will be permanent. It will be written in heaven and earthly governments will not be able to change it because they will not have the power to do so. We will be able to change the course of water. We will be able to change the growth patterns of grass. We will be able to change the appearance of animals. (Mark 11:23).

Do you realise that they knew about a type of gene technology called selective breeding in the Old Testament? Jacob took a stick and put it in the paddock, and all the sheep became streaked, speckled and spotted. *"And Jacob took rods of green poplar and of the almond and chestnut tree and peeled white strakes in them and made the white appear which was in the rods. And he set the rods which he had peeled before the flocks in the gutters in the watering troughs when the flocks came to drink, that they should conceive when they came to drink. And the flocks conceived before the rods, and brought forth flocks striped, speckled, and spotted."* (Genesis 30:37-39). You need to understand what that stick was. It was the government of YHVH because Jacob knew about being in heaven. He brought heaven to bear on earth to change the genomes of the sheep in the womb of their mother. Then, suddenly, Laban decided he wanted all of them. So Jacob set in place another stick and all the sheep became another color (Gen 31:8). It is in the Bible, gene technology out of heaven. That is power, legislative power.

The king and priest together form an arc

YHVH is releasing both the king and priest (Revelation 1:6). The role of the Melchizedek priest is to be the burden bearer of the human race. The priest corresponds to the Ox face of YHVH. I have a teaching called the *Four Faces of God* (see Realms of the Kingdom Volume 2 Trading in the Heavns). The Ox (priest) is the burden bearer that carries the weight of responsibility. The king is about the Lion of YHVH that is going to roar. Everything will know that there is something else in government. Something other than what we have presently assigned in that nation. When the Lion speaks, or when we speak from heaven, it is going to thunder on the earth. This is going to change everything.

The oracle and legislator on the earth

The king and priest are a heavenly involvement that forms an arc for the reflection on the earth to take on the expression of it. This is so that it can be revealed in the earth through the legislator (YHVH's man face) and the oracle. So when we take the legislative power of a king (Lion), with papers, it will come through the mouth of the oracle (YHVH's Eagle). It will be spoken: "This will happen today!" and it will happen. Because of our seat in heaven, we will speak and it WILL come to pass. And in that day, you will say to that mountain, "You! Move here!" (Matthew 21:21; Mark 11:23) and it will move. It does not have a choice.

The apostolic was supposed to function like the Melchizedek legislator

The apostolic is a really interesting governmental mantle. The apostolic was not supposed to be a mountain of personal power. Men have frequently made it a mountain. Many people want to become apostles because that is the head of the food chain. Those who used to be teachers became prophets and those who were prophets became apostles. In Christ, you can function in all five anyway, so I do not really know why anyone would choose only one. That is really a bit of a waste of time when all five are effectively available to you in Christ, even though your motivation might primarily be out of only one.

The apostolic was supposed to carry a blueprint of heaven. Everybody was supposed to be engaged with the blueprint, not engaged with the person or a mountain. Everyone in the church was supposed to be given a role or function. They were supposed to be empowered to become a reflection of heaven under the apostolic government. But the apostolic has often been built into a ministry in which you pay to belong to a network and they become your covering. These are just my thoughts regarding what we have and are trading with. I do not mind people having partners to co- labor with them as long as they do not actually come *under them.* They co-labor *with* you, for the sake of the blueprint, to fulfill the mandate of YHVH on the earth. Yeshua has the final blueprint and we all need to be walking in that blueprint.

The function of the Legislator is to find the blueprint of YHVH, to lay it out and then empower people to come into that blueprint. The Oracle's function is to teach about the blueprint, to speak about the mystery of the blueprint and then to help mature sons to come into the fullness of the measure of Christ, the stature of YHVH, within the blueprint. That is what the true apostolic should have been doing but maybe has not always done that. There are a few people on the earth who have been walking in some of this. So often those of a previous age who had the power will fight against change especially if they have become irrelevant and the power base is gone. In the Order of Melchizedek, the legislator and the oracle are the earthly manifestation. They are the practical grinding out into the earth of the two heavenly offices of king and priest. So, when you are in heaven on earth, you can bring heaven into the shadow of what is formed on the earth as the king and priest. Then heaven will manifest itself though the legislator and oracle. These are the four faces of the order of Melchizedek that we are going to walk in, in full measure, in the days to come.

Our four faces will manifest the glory of heaven into all creation

We will be increasingly known as a priest and king, a legislator and an oracle of the mouth piece of YHVH. Through us, these four faces will manifest the glory of heaven in fullness on the earth and into our solar system, into our galaxy and into the universe. Remember, it must always start in Jerusalem (the earth). The glory of the Lord must start in the house. Then it will flow from the house into everything else that is around it. It will flow into our solar system, into the twelve houses in heaven, into our galaxy and then into the rest of the galaxies. It will fill the universe with the light and the glory of the countenance of YHVH shining from the earth once again. The earth is the centre piece of the Father's plans.

Governmental power will again come from the centre of the earth

NASA sent a spaceship out into space and, after many years, they turned and took a camera shot with the earth in the middle. You can see this on Google. The full photograph took something like four years to get back because it was so dense with pixels. When they assembled it, they found an astonishing thing. There was a beam of light coming from top to bottom. In the centre of that beam of light was only one planet, the earth. No other star or planet was in this shaft of light that ran right through the centre of the picture. Yet it had millions of stars around it. The earth is this little blue dot sitting right in the centre of it.

Everything out there is looking at you, saying, "Get your act together". You need to know that YHVH wants you to come into the fullness of sonship and walk into the age of Melchezidek ,so that we can experience what it means to be at the centre of it again. It is from the centre that government is going to flow outward because you have power in the middle, not on the outside. That is why we have power in the middle, not on the outside. So, from within us, it is going to come in the same way as it is from the centre of the earth. The power is going to come from the centre of the earth again when we understand the seat of the government that sits in the middle of the earth. And, from that, we can bring divine order into everything again.

YHVH has got a plan and He is not out of time. He is very happy with the process because He has looked to this day as have many men and women. They have looked to this day and have said, "We want a part." And we have a part of it today.

Activation

Hallelujah. Glory.

Father, we want to thank You for the testimony of the Son of God that made a way. He was the Firstborn, who would receive judgment so that we could be the second-born, to receive grace to enable us to walk in the grace of the measure of the Firstborn.

Father, I ask for great grace to be assigned to men and women who do not understand what we have talked about. I ask that over this next year, You would begin to engage them and to release truth to bring understanding about who they really are.

I ask, Father, that You would bring revelation into our lives about who we really are and that You would make it really plain and easy for us to see and understand.

Lord, we want to attest today that You are Lord.

Yeshua, we declare that You are Lord to the glory of YHVH the Father. We declare that at Your name and in Your name, every knee will bow, every tongue will confess that Jesus Christ is Lord to the glory of God the Father.

Lord, today we want to confess that you are Lord. We say, "Yeshua, You are Lord."

Lord, today we want to make a fresh commitment to Your presence, to pursue You with Passion, Fire, and Glory. Lord, we ask that this bench of three would begin to rule over our lives to bring us into the fullness of the sons of God so that we would be revealed on the earth, in our day, in the measure of Melchizedek.

In the name of Yeshua HaMashiach, Anokhi[11], Elohim YHVH. Shalom.

[11] Anokhi meaning "I Am" in Hebrew found in: Matt 22:32, Mk. 12:26, Acts 7:32 referring to Exodus 3:6

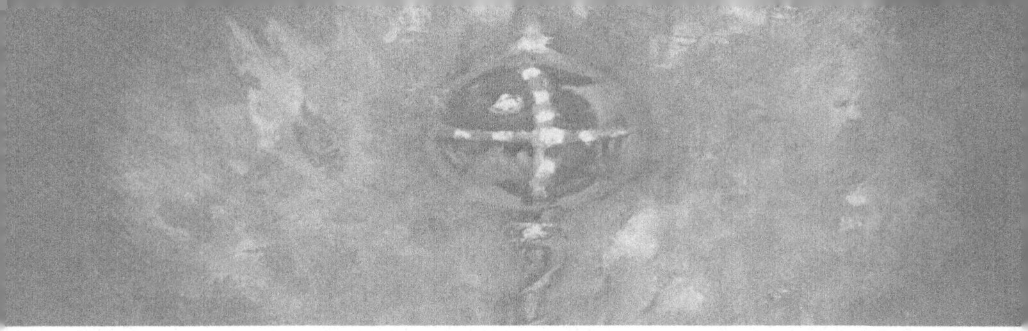

Chapter 8

The Pattern

There is an innate desire in every single one of us to create. We need to understand that if we are going to be a priest over something and a king over something, to have a voice and bring government into it, we must understand how it was made.

We are limited concerning the process of creation because we are bound in the atmosphere of the earth. The realm that YHVH wants us to engage with is in His world. When we go into His world we come outside of the confinements of the temple we live in and the restrictions here in the physical. We then see the truth of what is really there and the potential we have. It cannot be found on this side of the veil.

I have been going down a pathway talking about the veil on purpose for many years. I have been talking about it being rent and opened up. We need to go to the realm which is within the veil to get an understanding of how to create life. That life is not created this side of the veil. You and I are called to create it there then bring it into this realm and manifest it here because *you* are the Voice of what is within the veil. The problem with us is that we get confined into this physical realm here. We look at ourselves in the mirror with all our faults and failings and we think, "I am just a pathetic little human being – a human doing".

The Pattern of Atoms

Quantum physics has shown us just how amazing atoms are. If you were to take out the space between the nucleus of every atom and the electrons buzzing around the outside of it, the earth would compact down to about the size of a soccer ball – a very heavy soccer ball! That is why a planet forms a black hole when it collapses. All the space between the atoms gets crushed as it implodes and what you are left with is a solid mass with huge gravity around the outside of it.

If we were to take out the space between the nucleus and the electrons inside of you, you would contain ninety-nine percent 'empty space'. Actually, all you might be is a hologram of a reality that is going to pass away. You are empty space because there is so little solid material. To create mass we have to take out that 'empty space' gap. The only way to take out that gap is to go back to the very Source of the origins of the framework that created the gap and we do have access to that Source.

There is coming a day when we are going to be able to create things. These things will never have to be built because your desire will bring a framework to the testimony that opens up this realm so that the physical world will respond to that desire. So you and I will frame up something that was not there before.

It is your desire that brings the framework for hope to materialise what faith believes is possible. You have got to have faith and hope, they are the RNA of heaven. RNA is the building block that sets every material thing in place to be able to hold it together in the framework. Without RNA there is no framework for something that is physical. Without RNA you would just be a blob floating around. RNA is our *'revealed nature achieved'*.

DNA is *'the divine nature assimilated'*. So without *Divine Nature Assimilated* and *Revealed Nature Achieved* in you, you will not be able to realise substance out of nothing. This "nothing" is already here in the spirit world. It is just not visible. Everything we need for our physical wellbeing is in the atmosphere already, but because we cannot see it, most of us do not believe it is there. Most of us are taught to only engage and look at the physical world. So most people do not engage the spirit world, and the Kingdom world, which has everything present already inside of it. Many of us are living in chaos because we are only looking at the physical world.

What is hope? The bible says, "... *faith is the substance of things hoped for, the evidence of things not seen*" (Hebrews 11:1). So faith is a tangible reality of things dreamed about that are yet in vision form. The capacity of *desire* is what creates vision form. When you desire something you look at it, you frame it up, you engage it, you empower it and then you will precipitate it around your life. Whatever you are hoping for in your life, and whatever you look at, that is what will frame your testimony of the future. That also includes the destructive things. If you are worried about the future then you are framing up chaos into it. Many of us are so worried about what is coming to the earth. That is because we have not seen in heaven what is coming to us from heaven. Do not worry about your future. If YHVH can care for the stars, do you not think He can give you enough to care for your day? You need to know YHVH has got it well in hand.

YHVH's pattern is scientific

So let us return to atoms. If we have a tree and you set fire to it and it burns away so there is nothing left but dust, every single atom of that tree still exists. Those atoms have not gone anywhere; they are now just in a different pattern. That means if we found the pattern we could remake the tree, because the pattern sets the parameters of the boundary for the formation of matter out of atoms.

We need to understand that YHVH is a scientist. When you understand how YHVH made something, you can find the pattern and you can remake it. With the burnt tree there is a pattern of something that actually still exists but now its vibrational frequency is in a different pattern. It has now changed and all those atoms are just 'out there' somewhere.

To re-form the tree, what we need is the pattern of the Voice that holds that tree together. That Voice is only found in the Father. It is not found because you want it. So the only way to create light and to create matter out of nothing is to be *in* the Father. In John 17:21, Jesus says, *"That they all may be one; as you, Father, are in me, and I in you, that they also may be one in us."* This means that I am in the Father, in Jesus, because Jesus said He and the Father are one. If I am in the Father, then I have an intrinsic ability in my Father, from my position in Him, to be able to create matter. If we are to learn to create, our issue is to find how to make the jigsaw puzzle come back together. That is a problem because every atom has a mind of its own. That is until a sound is made that forms a frequency that attracts it to its original pattern.

Where do physical healings come from? They come from you framing atoms out of a material substance that is not visible. No one can see atoms in the air even though they are there. You cannot see them because they are not in a framework that our bodies are used to interacting with but your spirit man is. Your spirit man is used to interacting with the framework of heaven. The framework of heaven in the physical world is the atoms that are invisible to the naked eye.

YHVH has given us the intrinsic ability to create matter and it is fun creating! That is why we get stuck on healings, and we get stuck on all this creating things because it is exciting to watch it happen. But if you are just healing the sick and you are not engaging the testimony of the universe you have got a problem because you are only believing what you see in front of you, not what you do not see out there. The whole of creation is waiting for us to get our act together. "… *We know that all creation has been groaning as in the pains of childbirth right up to the present time. And we believers also groan, even though we have the Holy Spirit within us as a foretaste of future glory, for we long for our bodies to be released from sin and suffering. We, too, wait with eager hope for the day when God will give us our full rights as his adopted children, including the new bodies he has promised us*" (Romans 8:22 – 23).

As part of who we are as sons of YHVH, He has given us the intrinsic ability to create mass out of light and power. That is why we are called *"children of light"* (1 Thessalonians 5:5, Ephesians 5:8). That is why we have got to *"walk in the light"* (1 John 1:7). That is why we have to be *"in the light"* (1 John 1:7). When we understand the intrinsic value of light, then we can understand that the power in light can form mass.

When a baby comes out of the womb, it is born out of creative light[12] in full awareness of all of the glory of YHVH because its spirit man has not yet been shut down. That baby coming from the womb is born into darkness. The created light coming from the sun is darkness. We are:

born into darkness,
to see the light,
to walk in the light,
to become a reflection of light,
to bear the image of light,
and to become light.

The end must always equal the beginning. This is a scriptural law and one of the twelve Laws of Zion. Where we have come from is what we are going to look like. We are going to look exactly the same at the end as we were in the beginning if we engage and believe YHVH for the truth of our testimony because we are being changed "from glory to glory, even as by the Spirit of the Lord" (2 Corinthians 3:18). This is because you and I already hold all of that inside of us. Your spirit man already has full awareness of all of this; it is not new. Just because you have not heard it before does not mean you do not know it. You already have full knowledge of all of creation because you were in the Father before you were in the earth. *"Before I formed you in the womb I knew you"* (Jeremiah 1:5). *"God chose us to be in a relationship with Him even before He laid out plans for this world"* (Ephesians 1:4 VOICE). Now you are on the earth coming back into the Father, which is coming back into the full knowledge of what you already knew anyway. "I *will be there to greet you personally and welcome you home, where we will be together. You know where I am going and how to get there"* (John 14:3-4 VOICE).

Einstein was Jewish. He found the formula $E=mc^2$, from creation. When we transpose it we obtain $m=E/c^2$ which is the formula to create mass. In Jewish mystical tradition it is said to

[12] The concept of creative vs created light is explained in Realms of the Kingdom Volumes 1 and 2

also be the formula for the first letter of the Hebrew alphabet, the *Aleph*.

Hebrew meaning of 'Adam'

When YHVH made man He called him 'Adam', which is Hebrew for 'man'.

The word *A-da-m* consists of three Hebrew letters: *Aleph*, *Dalet* and *Mem*.

There are many deeper revelatory interpretations of these letters. This is a simplified version[13].

Aleph א came from a picture of an ox head. It means *government (power and authority)*.

Dalet ד *was developed from* a picture of a door and it means *door.*

Mem מ started off as a picture of waves of water or a river flowing. It means *a river of supply*.

So, the name *Adam* means: *the head of a door flowing with life, the government of a door to the river of supply*.

We are 'Adam'

YHVH wants us to come into the process of understanding that we are *Adam*. That means that we have the capacity and the ability to be the governing way for *the Voice* of YHVH through the testimony of heaven. The name *'Adam'* enables you to be a door for all of that power and all of that light to come as a never-ending supply. It sets you to govern a river flowing out of your life into the world that is around you. It empowers you to terraform and to change the sound and frequency of the earth until it comes back into its original pattern.

Going a little bit deeper, did YHVH make everything? Yes, *"All things were made by him; and without him was not anything made that was made"* (John 1:3). Is YHVH in everything? Yes, *"One*

[13] Note that this refers to the pictures for these letters in ancient Hebrew, which grew into the modern letters we study today.

God and Father of all, who is above all, and through all, and in you all" (Ephesians 4:6). Are you in YHVH? Yes, *"I am in My Father, you are in Me, and I am in you"* (John 14:20 TLV). So, if I am in YHVH and YHVH is in everything, then everything has a sound for *my* pattern to fit into that will respond to it. If I am in YHVH and YHVH is in all of creation, and there is a testimony of YHVH in everything that has been created, then everything in creation is designed to respond to the DNA of *'Adam'*. Therefore man's job is to bring life into all of eternity. All of creation is waiting for your revelation, waiting for *Adam* to show up *"For the creation eagerly awaits the revelation of the sons of God"* (Romans 8:19 TLV). This means not just one little galaxy or one little solar system. Satan really messed up our solar system and we are going to terraform it and bring it back to the way it was in the first place.

We happen to live in one of the smallest solar systems situated on a spiral arm of a small galaxy that only spans 100,000 light years across. There are some galaxies that span up to 6 million light years across. Do you think that in over two trillion galaxies spanning perhaps 93 billion light years across there are no other creatures?

The problem is that, through Adam, we are the ones that brought corruption and darkness into the universe. But through Christ, we are the ones that are going to bring incorruption and light back into the universe. So, if you do not want your galaxy, I will have it. If you do not want to sit on your throne in the middle of a dark hole, I will have it. The reason a black hole exists is because there is no creative light radiating out of it, so everything that is created light is going into it to try and find creative light.

Numerical meaning of 'Adam'

Each letter in the Hebrew alphabet also represents a number. So Adam's name actually adds up to nine.

In Ezekiel 28:13, Lucifer had nine different stones all over him: "*...every precious stone was your covering, the sardius, topaz, and the diamond, the beryl, the onyx, and the jasper, the sapphire, the emerald,* *and the carbuncle...*" YHVH covered him with stones.

Nine is interesting because it contains three lots of *three*. 'Three' represents government. The number three is significant in the Word: Father, Son and Holy Spirit each has three 'skins' or three aspects or layers of their natures:

Jesus the Son: the Way, the Truth and the Life (John 14:6)
Holy Spirit: righteousness, peace and joy (Romans 14:17)
The Father: judgment, justice and holiness (Isaiah 5:16)

- We have three physical layers of skin.
- The earth has three main physical layers.
- The sun's atmosphere has three physical layers in it.

You: have a body, soul and spirit.

When your 'three' are added to the three lots of *three* of Father, Son and Holy Spirit it makes *twelve:*

- The priest had twelve stones on his breastplate (Exodus 28:21).
- There are twelve houses in heaven and twelve gates of the new Jerusalem (Revelation 21:13).
- There are twelve tribes of Israel (Genesis 49:28).

Twelve is a picture of government because there must be a formation of the truth of our testimony. Government is established in Adam's name both numerically and in the meaning of the Hebrew letters.

The pattern of the *Voice*

Hebrews 11:3 says, "*...the worlds were framed by the word of God...*" So we need to understand *'The Voice'* because when you are <u>in</u> the Voice, speaking from <u>within</u> the Voice, you can frame matter.

When YHVH speaks, He sends out:

- the mathematical equation
- the colour

- the frequency
- the song
- the fragrance
- the scroll of testimony

He releases everything all at once.

In John 6:40, Yeshua says, *"And this is the will of him that sent me, that everyone who sees the Son, and believes on him, may have everlasting life: and I will raise him up at the last day."* Those that *see* Me, (not just *Hear* Me), and believe in Me will have everlasting life. The church has taught us how to *hear*, not how to *see*. You can find thousands of books on how to hear the *Voice* of God. All you are hearing is a miniscule piece of the Voice. If you really heard the Voice, you would create what the Voice has said. We are very selective in what we are hearing because we mainly use it for direction. That is why people pray: they want to learn direction. So they pray, pray, pray, 'to hear the voice of God'. Then they write it down. This is all good exercise because it helps you hear a little tiny piece of what heaven is saying. When YHVH speaks, He speaks *everything* into creation! This provides the full potential for it to be fully manifested and fully revealed in its fullness in the physical environment in order to create matter out of energy and light.

Hebrew letters are a door into what YHVH has spoken

One of the things I love about the Hebrew language is that it is mathematical. It is one of the only languages in the world that can be mapped mathematically and you can use it to create formulae in science. That is why Albert Einstein and those other early scientists who did fantastic revelatory things on the face of the earth were all Jewish. They understood *The Voice.* Once you understand the *pattern* of *The Voice,* you can understand science. The Hebrew language is a scientific and mathematical language. All of creation is woven into it. That is why each letter has a meaning in it. That meaning is for a specific reason. It speaks of something of its own. If each letter stood on its own it would actually speak of itself. The *Aleph,* in a sense, speaks "$m=E/c^2$".

When YHVH writes things down, (as in heaven when a scroll is given to you and the scroll is opened), the letters are free to come off. They are not written like you and I write them. They are a record of a door of revelation. You need to go through this door to see the fullness of the breadth and depth and height of what YHVH has spoken.

Sometimes seeing something in the natural world can help you understand something of the spirit world.

Einstein's equation: $E = mc^2$.

Because he was Jewish, Einstein understood about creation and found his formula from creation. He tried to teach the world about creation and being able to create matter or mass out of energy and light. Einstein's equation ($E=mc^2$) shows us how to produce mass. Mass is actually: $m=E/c^2$ where m is mass, E is energy, and c is the speed of light. So, energy divided by the speed of light squared produces mass ($E/c^2=m$).

What is energy? Energy is *Power*! It is the ultimate power trip because it is inexhaustible and totally replenishable. Energy does not contain or confine itself to the medium of *created* things. It is in the *uncreated* world. It is also in the *invisible* realm within the created world. There are atoms here in the created world that you cannot see because they are invisible to the naked eye, but they are still here; we just pass straight through them.

And so, to understand the spirit world of YHVH, we need to try and figure out what $E=mc^2$ really means. If science discovered $E=mc^2$, then YHVH must have spoken $E=mc^2$ into existence because science only engages what has already been created.

Aleph at the very beginning

Let us look at the first letter of the Hebrew alphabet because this is believed to be instrumental in how creation was made. As we said, $m=E/c^2$ can be seen in a spiritual sense as the formula for the *Aleph*. We need to understand that the foundation of something comes from a right beginning. That is why the

Lamb of God was slain *before* the foundation of the world. (Revelation 13:8; 1 Peter 1:19-20). It began all the way back there. It began in light and in eternity. This became a pinpoint that opened up like a balloon that expanded into our universe with the Voice creating matter. The Voice moves many times faster than the speed of light, some have said, actually ten thousand times faster than the speed of light, because it is the speed of thought. The speed of thought travelling between the neurons in your brain moves many times faster than the speed of light.

When you look at the letter *Aleph* א as a Hebrew character, it has actually got three Hebrew symbols or letters within it. When you break it down it has a *Vav* ו and two *Yods* י . The letter *Aleph* can also been seen as a picture of YHVH *speaking.* It is the foundation of government. At the very beginning, YHVH spoke; and at the very beginning, He created. The Hebrew letter *Aleph* is at the very beginning, it is the beginning of everything. Aleph is the governmental Voice of YHVH that frames the universe. So, materializing matter is just actually Aleph. It is the presiding governmental Voice of YHVH that frames the complete universe. The letter "A" in English means absolutely nothing because it is not connected to anything. But the letter *Aleph* means a whole lot more.

The letter *Mem* looks similar to a diagram of the firmament with waters above and beneath. Interestingly, to a Hebrew this means: '*What*' and '*Is*'. You have the 'upper water' (the '*What*') and the 'lower water' (the '*Is*').

Genesis 1:7 says, "*...God separated the waters...*" So He put an expanse above which carried His Voice and He put an expanse below which was where the creativity of YHVH was to be expressed through man to create heaven on earth. The '*What*' is all that is out there that we do *not* see. The '*Is*' is all that we *do* see. So if we engage and live in the '*What*' then, out of the '*What*', we can conform the '*Is*' to the '*What*'. I know this takes a bit of wrapping your head around but I want to pick up this thing here with the *Aleph* and to talk more about this *Upper* and the *Lower* to help us understand our position. We are in the earth, which is the under *or* the lower, but our position is in the upper because that is really where we are seated in Christ. *"But God, who is rich in mercy, for his great love with which he loved us, Even when we were dead in sins, has made us alive together with Christ, (by grace you are saved;) And has raised us up together, and made us sit together in heavenly places in Christ Jesus"* (Ephesians 2:4-6). We are in the upper.

We read in Genesis, *"In the beginning God created the heavens and the earth. Now the earth was chaos and waste, darkness was on the surface of the deep, and the Ruach Elohim was hovering upon the surface of the water"* (Genesis 1:1-2 TLV). The Father brooded (or hovered) over the face of the deep, the upper was brooding over the lower, to bring the lower into conformity with the image of the upper. Holy Spirit was brooding over it. That word *brood* means 'to vibrate'. Holy Spirit was vibrating over the lower, and bringing it into the same harmony as the upper, so that the lower could bear the same image as the upper. In churches we say to God, "Jesus, come down," and He does not come down. "Holy Spirit, fill the room," and He does not fill the room. This is because we have not been in the upper and understood the essence of who we are in the upper, to empower the lower to take on the image of the upper. Only when the lower takes on the image of the upper will the upper respond to the lower. Until the lower looks like the upper, the upper cannot acknowledge the lower as its own.

One of the key issues regarding us as believers is that we have seen ourselves in the lower. We do not see ourselves in the upper. That is because we are told we are unworthy to go there. We say: "Only one day when we die will we see it all. Only one day when we die will we ever be sinless. Only one day when we die will we ever be able to overcome our enemy. Only one day when we die..." You know the scenario.

Yet we want all of that which is in the upper down here in the lower. But we cannot bring it down here because we have not spent the time in the upper to take on the sound of the testimony of that Voice's framework there, to bring that down here so that the witness on earth will be as it is in heaven. The

Bible does not say, "*In heaven* as it is *on earth*". No, it says, "*Your Kingdom come. Your will be done in earth, as it is in heaven*" (Matthew 6:10). There is a big struggle in churches today refraining from teaching people how to go into the upper. People are taught how to *hear* the voice of God instead of *seeing* the Person of YHVH by leaders who do not want you to be in the upper, nor do they want to go there themselves. They know that the moment you get into a higher place than they are, they lose their power over your life.

When we look at the process of changing something, we go into the What, and then out of the '*What*' the '*Is*' is formed. To form matter we have got to be in the what. We have got to position ourselves in that realm of the Father where His Voice is continually creating so we see what the Voice is doing. Then we stand down here and we become the Voice. Because we have seen what the Voice is doing, we become the Voice, and we create material matter out of the 'What' into the '*Is*'. That is why Matthew 6:10 says, '*On earth as it is in heaven*'. But you cannot do it on earth unless you are in heaven.

The pattern that YHVH has spoken has never stopped forming. It continues doing what it did in the very beginning and it has never stopped. We have an expanding universe.

To learn what is going on in the beginning

Our job is to learn what is happening. But we have got to go into the '*What*' to find out what is going on at the beginning because the end of the universe is still the beginning of something new. For example, if we have a balloon expanding, each part of the balloon is still the beginning.

For us to change what '*Is*' we have got to go to the beginning. It is only at the beginning that you will get the purity and essence of the creative wind of the Voice of YHVH. Then we bring that Voice back into our day to recreate and reform what '*Is*' here. I have been to the edge and I have seen it. I have experienced it and I have grown a galaxy. The Father is inviting us to do these things so we can understand what we are really supposed to be doing. It took me four and half hours at thought speed to get to the edge of the universe and it is wonderful! I am not saying I am any better than anyone else. I am just saying, take a chance – you can go there. It is the most wonderful thing.

We have to understand the *pattern* to materialise matter

When we understand the pattern we can materialise anything into the atmosphere but, to understand the pattern, we have got to know the *Voice*. To know the *Voice* we need to be where the *Voice* is and, to be where the *Voice* is, we have got to go to where the *Voice* is and stand in that *Voice*, to watch what the *Voice* does, so when you stand down here you can do what the *Voice* is doing. "*...whoever believes in me will do the same things that I do. Those who believe will do even greater things than these, because I am going to the Father...*" (John 14:12 EXB).

Whenever we find patterns they are important. With the structure of matter things work in fours. We have atoms, molecules, particles, and then we have matter. To form matter you need to have the pattern of the particles. To form particles you have got to actually have the substance of molecules and know how they fit together. To have the substance of the molecules, you need to have an idea of the atoms.

And there are so many atoms to form one pattern. The possibility has too many zeros to even be able to write it down. The formula would reach from here to beyond the sun with a nought every half inch. Think about finding just one molecule in the pattern of how to make a tree. Positioning that molecule in the jigsaw puzzle to form a tree would also have noughts all the way to the sun! That is just one molecule, one tiny piece of the jigsaw puzzle!

However, if you actually have that pattern, you can fit them all together like a jigsaw puzzle. If you were to collapse all the spaces between them, then all you have left is the actual substance, the material matter that is in the centre of a particle. That is why the Word says the worlds were framed, and then YHVH breathed into them and created life. "*... The worlds were framed by the word of God, so that things which are seen were not* *made of things which do appear"* (Hebrews 11:3). He created life by increasing the space between the atoms.

One of the amazing examples of a pattern is how the cells of the body copy themselves. It starts with twenty-two autosomes and one sex chromosome from the father, plus twenty-two autosomes and one sex chromosome from the mother. When they come together they form this little DNA-thing. Suddenly it divides into two, then four, eight, sixteen… It starts to multiply exponentially but it is all following a specific pattern.

Do you realise that if you found one pattern you could recreate all of creation? The only place you find that pattern is at the beginning.

I am sorry that this is so scientific, but to understand how the Order of Melchizedek works, you need to understand this.

Kings have huge responsibility: their words create

We really have to get to grips with this. To understand you are a king is to understand that there is a *responsibility*. As a king, you have judicial rights to create matter, to perform the works that YHVH did, to bear His image in the earth in the fullness, so that all of what is known in creation can know your face.

To understand the responsibility is to understand that your words will create. We are going to be held to account for every idle word because your words *will* create. "… *every idle word that men shall speak, they shall give account thereof in the day of judgment" (Matthew 12:36)*. When we come into a position of government whatever we say *will* come to pass. As we stand in that place as a king, a priest, an oracle and a legislator, moving in Four Faces[14], our words *will* create. I am talking about responsibility. I want to help you to understand that when you only have wisdom and understanding as Lucifer did in Ezekiel 28:4, but without the knowledge of YHVH, you will create chaos. *"With your wisdom and with your understanding you have gotten yourself riches, and have gotten gold and silver into your treasuries: By your great wisdom*

[14] See the four faces of God, in Realms of the Kingdom Volume 2 Trading in the heavens

and by your trade have you increased your riches, and your heart is lifted up because of your riches" (Ezekiel 28:4-5).

Yeshua opened up the pattern so we could go back to the beginning

And so, we need the knowledge which is at the very beginning because knowledge sets the pattern. So we need to go back to the beginning. The priest's job was to go back to the beginning. The high priest would go in with the blood of oxen and sheep. Jesus did the same thing with His own blood.

"*When the Anointed One arrived as High Priest of the good things that are to come, He entered through a greater and more perfect sanctuary that was not part of the earthly creation or made by human hands. He entered once for all time into the most holy place – entering, not with the blood of goats or calves or some other prescribed animal, but offering His own blood and thus obtaining redemption for us for all time*" (Hebrews 9:11-12 VOICE).

We do not have to use the blood of oxen and sheep. We can go through into that pattern by the blood of Jesus. Jesus opened up the pattern so we could go back to the beginning because He is the beginning and the end. *"I am Alpha and Omega, the beginning and the end, the first and the last"* (Revelation 22:13). So we can go back to the very beginning. For a Hebrew, everything is circular because the beginning must equal the end. "*For just as the days of Noah were, so will be the coming of the Son of Man*" (Matthew 24:37 TLV).

The reason that this circular motion exists is because when you come back to the very beginning, you see the end of everything as well. When you see the *end* of everything it is totally complete. This means you can engage something completely new and recreate the very beginning – in your day. If you look at a point on a circle, the beginning and the end are right there beside each other. The past can be one second that side of yesterday, or one second past the second that has just gone past a second ago. All of the past is contained in a second away from you, and all of the future is a second in front of you.

Our job is to reach the *end* of the beginning of the matter, so that we can understand the fullness of the pattern of what we need to do to create the beginning of a matter. If there is chaos and destruction when I am at the *end* of something, then I need to create something at the beginning that will reform it in a totally different fashion.

The *pattern* of His *Voice* in us terraforms

I have put this in print so you can keep re-reading it. You are powerful enough to throw it all out of the window if you choose to. I am teaching this so that we can get to the point where YHVH can begin to trust us with the pattern of His Voice. Once you have the pattern of the *Voice*, you will create matter in every single circumstance of your life.

I have been into the year 2057 and, by the way, the earth is still here. It looks different. There is a lot that is different and we function a little bit differently than we do now. But we will create. We will never have to build because all this that I am teaching here is fully understood by the sons. We will bring Eden back into the earth again and re-culture the earth in its original pattern because we will have access back into the *Way* of the Tree of Life. The Tree of Life is the realm of eternity where Eden is. This is called "terraforming" This means a new earth and a new heaven. (Revelation 21:1).The old heaven and old earth *will* pass away, (Revelation 6:14), which means it is not going to be destroyed. It is just going to become something completely new because the sense of pass away here means to be *re-born.*

YHVH is rotating around a new, far better dispensation

This pattern becomes very important – the circular motion of the way Hebrew people think is crucial for us. Several years ago, the Lord gave me a vision about what I was to do. He said something quite specific to me and I said, "Yes, Lord I will do that." Then He showed me the big picture and where certain land was situated. I said with excitement, "I am in! But I am not going to build in debt. You must provide or I am not going to build. It is as simple as that. It needs to be to the glory of

YHVH, debt free, because I am not going to be enslaved to anything." So I began to pray over this thing. I have talked a little about it elsewhere.

Well, that land was for sale for nearly four years. It did not sell. I went around it. praying, and I drove stakes into the ground and said, "Lord You told me this belongs to me", because He had shown me.

Three years and nine months later, the land sold. The person who owns it now will not sell it. So I could either say, "I did not hear right. Therefore the last four years of my life have been a waste of time, or else YHVH is doing something different."

If I think circular, it means YHVH is coming around to the beginning again. The next time around, it is going to be *greater* than it could have been the first time around. The latter glory is going to be greater than the former glory (Haggai 2:9). So, the Lord had shown me a former glory. That has come around to completion and that time line has now passed. Now YHVH is rotating around a whole new dispensation and it is far better than it was before.

But I could have rejected it and said: "Aw! I did not hear the Lord. I am just a waste of time. And I am a silly nucleus of a Christian trying to live my life as a Christian on the face of the earth." No! Forget that. YHVH's dream does not change, it just gets better. That is why the Father's dream about what we would do has never changed, it has just got better and bigger. We need to engage some of these things so that YHVH can bring to pass what He wants on the face of the earth.

Atoms contain the voice of YHVH

Let's return to the subject of patterns and the *Voice* to lay a better understanding for what the Order of Melchizedek involves.

We need to understand how atoms form together. They are framed with the voice of YHVH in them. That forms a pattern of every single created thing. We must frame ourselves in YHVH: *Yod, Hey, Vav, Hey.*[15] Then we can stand at the very

[15] Yod, Hey, Vav, Hey are the four Hebrew letters used to represent God's name

beginning of the point of time and begin to create matter around us. We can begin to change the sound of the frequency of everything around us. We can reform it into its original constitution, the way it should have been before the fall. We are then going to terraform it because we will have a pattern.

With power comes responsibility

There is huge responsibility that comes with knowing the pattern. You are going to be responsible for everything you create. That is why Yeshua is called the first-born of many (Colossians 1:15), and that is why He was slain at the very beginning (Revelation 13:8). When you begin to create something, you are going to have to be prepared to die for it because with power comes responsibility. It is not just a one-way, worship/glory trip. It is hard work because you have got to *brood* over it. In the same way, Adam was given dominion over the whole earth (Genesis 1:26), to brood over it. Adam ruled from the *centre* of the earth, because to make something small enough to be able to encompass it, you have to go to the centre.

It is amazing how the earth seems to be on this massive, big scale, and we think that it is huge. Actually it is really, really small when you go to the centre. It is not very big at all. That is how *one man* could have dominion over the *whole earth*. "*... and God said unto them, Be fruitful, and multiply, and fill the earth, and subdue it: and have dominion over the fish of the sea, and over the fowl of the air, and over every living thing that moves upon the earth.*" (Genesis 1:28). You must rule from the middle. That is how we are going to have dominion over a complete galaxy, because we will rule from the centre.

The *Voice* will re-create life

The pattern of the Voice of YHVH is important for us. The *Voice* is not just a spoken thing, like words coming out of my mouth. It is a formula to completely re-create life in a person's experience. It has fragrance, it has song – a sound. It has light and colour. It has a mathematical equation and a scroll of testimony. It has everything in it – it has a pattern.

So, for you and me to stand in the pattern, we have to go to the beginning. Our job as priest is to go in, into His world, and from within the boundaries of that world we need to allow Him to take us to the very beginning where we can see the end of our life. That is how Moses could write about creation without seeing it. It is how he could write about his own death in the third person before it happened, because he went to the end. Because when he saw himself at the end, the end was only his beginning.

This life is just temporal. The 'end' of your life is just the beginning. So if you die, then that is just the beginning. If you do not die, you are already past the beginning. Are you getting this? We have to be a priest so we are able to stand at this point *here* (a single point on a circular time line) and function from this role in what YHVH has given us – to create things. As Jesus is the Priest forever after the order of Melchizedek (Hebrews 7:17), then we have to understand who Melchizedek is. We have to get to grips with the functionality of this new priesthood that YHVH is raising on the face of the earth.

It does not have anything to do with church, because in December 2012, the Apostolic Order gave way to the new dispensation YHVH is revealing.

"And he gave some, apostles; and some, prophets; and some, evangelists; and some, pastors and teachers; For the perfecting of the saints, for the work of the ministry, for the edifying of the body of Christ: till we all come in the unity of the faith, and of the knowledge of the Son of God, unto a perfect man, unto the measure of the stature of the fullness of Christ" (Ephesians 4: 11-14)

Through the Melchizedek Order YHVH is releasing the perfect

YHVH is releasing that which is perfect into the earth to raise sons so that they will have precedence in heaven. This is actually the function of the Order of Melchizedek. It will bring sons to maturity and perfection so that they actually have dominion over *all* the earth, not just in their little church.

I know that YHVH is doing something that is so different to everything that has ever been seen before. It is going to take a while for our brains to even try and catch up with this 'Order of Melchizedek' because the Melchizedek Order has circular thinking. It does not think 'Mountain,' it thinks 'Blueprint' because, like YHVH, it also moves with Four Faces: king, priest, legislator and oracle. (We will be looking at these roles in more detail later in the book).

YHVH says that His Word will come and He will bring forth fruit: some thirty-fold, some sixty-fold, and some a hundred-fold. *"But he that received seed in the good ground is he that hears the word, and understands it; who also bears fruit, and brings forth, some a hundredfold, some sixty, some thirty"* (Matthew 13:23). Actually, that should read '*ninety*' (if you were to follow the pattern: thirty, sixty, and ninety). So, within the *hundred,* there is a (hidden) ten percent that will only ever attain to the Order of Melchizedek, because there is a price. There is a price behind this: it means you no longer live but Christ lives in you. You will no longer live in the confinements of the earth but you will live within the boundaries of heaven.

If we were to draw four concentric circles, the large outer area would represent thirty-fold. This is the outer court. The next layer in represents another thirty–fold and is the inner court. The next thirty percent layer in represents the Holy Place, and within this, the very small circle in the centre represents ten percent which is Holy of Holies and 'on to perfection'.

I personally want to be in that feast. But do you realise that you have to walk through these other outer layers to come there?

The mighty ones

Before the fullness of this is manifested, something will begin to form on the face of the earth. These will be called the *mighty ones.* The mighty ones will begin to show the way for the Order of Melchizedek to have a seat of government. They will begin to make known, like John the Baptist did, the ways of the Lord.

"The voice of one crying in the wilderness, Prepare you the way of the Lord" (Matthew 3:3). And if their function has been found worthy, then they will be rewarded with the Four Faces of Melchizedek as well. There are children that are being born today that are going to be seeing and experiencing this. And we are going to think 'who are they?' when they are only six, seven or eight years old.

The old will fight the new

It is amazing because the Apostolic Order is going to fight against the Order of Melchizedek. It still wants the power because it has built a mountain to itself. Not everyone is like that but, predominately on the face of the earth, this is the way the structure is: "*You* come in and serve me under my covering." Instead of: "You come into the covering of the Holy Spirit and serve Him and together we labour to build the pattern of heaven on the earth."

YHVH is beginning to move differently in the face of the earth today. He is doing something that has never been seen before.

Living on the *Event Horizon*

The reason the Bible is sketchy about the future is because you and I are supposed to live on the *Event Horizon* of the ending and the beginning. Every day of our life we are to walk with YHVH, creating and forming the *pattern* in the earth. Then, all of creation can begin to see that there is a new *pattern* being formed. That is why all of creation is groaning for our revealing as a son (Romans 8:19, 22). But we have said: "Oh, look, it is a fully-fledged apostle!" Sonship has nothing to do with apostleship. The office of apostle is a function and a position *on earth* to bring the earthly house from chaos into order and has no position in heaven only sons do.

Patterns are so important for us. Knowing the Face of the *Voice* is vital for us. Concerning the whole process of what YHVH wants to do on the earth, we have never ever been this way before. The earth has never seen the fullness of what it is going to be like in this day. *"Eye has not seen, nor ear heard, neither have entered into the heart of man, the things which God has prepared for them that love him"* (1 Corinthians 2:9). Those that have gone before us have *seen* it because they are already *in* it.

Regularly, now, we have watchmen, the 'men in white linen', coming and saying to us, "Prepare yourself He is coming." That is why they are showing up in meetings. They sometimes come to visit and have a look because we talk about them. They come because they understand the pattern. The moment they hear their name, it is a pattern of heaven manifesting on earth. And when you frame it, you give them a gate of entry because there is a pattern. YHVH is going to do things that are really weird and unusual but it is going to be so exciting and so amazing!

A new circular dispensational period, living out of the future

We are entering into a complete, new circular dispensational period. We are living on the *Event Horizon*, or the *Rosenbridge* of life. From here you can see past your day into that which is in the future and then you can reach in there and bring it into your day. You can live out of the future because you have already seen the termination of it. That is why David could kill Goliath. That is why David could go and do the things he did, because he had seen into the future. How can someone kill you, even if you are only thirteen years of age, when you know you are the King of Israel?

When you know your future, your present cannot harm you. That is why Paul knew that nothing could harm him and he had to go to Jerusalem.

Paul writes: *"Five times from the Jewish leaders I received forty lashes minus one. Three times I was beaten with rods. Once I was stoned. Three times I suffered shipwreck"* (2 Corinthians 11:24-25 TLV). But he says, *"... in all these things we are more than conquerors through him that loved us"* (Romans 8:37). Why, because he had seen his end. Who can kill you when you know your end? But then, who can kill you when you know your beginning? We are coming into a new world, a new realm at the beginning.

Activation

Father, thank You that we are energy over the speed of light squared (E/c^2).

Thank You that You have given us the capacity to create life and to walk in Your mysteries.

Father, today, we open our heart and we ask You to do what is necessary to bring us to maturity, to be an expression of a government, of a door of a never-ending river of supply to all of creation.

Father, we want to walk in the fullness of that supply, to be on earth as we are in heaven.

We want to be in heaven and have that full expression of heaven in us, through us, around us, from us, and to us, of heaven in the earth.

Thank You for Your grace, Father, that You lead us.

Thank You Lord, that You change us so that the veil of our body would be rent, that our DNA would be torn and reveal the truth of the nature that is really hidden inside us.

Thank You Lord, for Your mercy.

Today, Father, we want to *shift*.

Lord, we want to *shift* into Your world, into Your Kingdom.

Father, as we stand *here* today, we ask that revelation would *govern* us, *engage* us and bring us into the reality of who we are in *the Upper*.

Father, we receive all that we need out of *Your* world today.

Father, we *receive* it today from Your Presence, because, Lord, this can only be found in Your Presence.

As we stand in Your Presence, Yeshua, we position ourselves in the *Name* of the Father. Father, we ask that You would begin to open up the world of the angelic, the world of the men in white linen. We ask that the whole mystical realm with Your Kingdom, Father, would begin to open up to us as Your sons.

Father, we receive the full provision of all that we need from *Your* Kingdom world to precipitate *this* world into *our* world.

Thank you, Lord, for your grace. In the name of Yeshua HaMashiach, Amen

Chapter 9
The Blueprint

"And as we have borne the image of the earthly, we shall also bear the image of the heavenly" (1 Corinthians 15:49).

I really find that when YHVH speaks, He does not speak into what we know. He speaks into what we do not know in the hope that we would be yoked to what we do not know, to understand how to get to what we do not know. How can we understand YHVH, who is beyond our understanding, even with the number of dimensions that we know about in the universe we live in? Trans-dimensionally, outside of that, there are many more dimensions.

We come as a three-dimensional being, moving into trying to get understanding of the function of a multi-dimensional transcendent God. When He moves we are often shocked because we try and figure it out in our little three-dimensional being's brain. When YHVH comes and He speaks into the earth, we often receive it on a platform very ill-prepared for all that He is saying.

Isaiah 2:3 says, *"Come, and let us go up to the mountain of the LORD… and he will teach us of his ways"*. We cannot understand the ways of YHVH on the earth. They can only be understood in heaven. That is why we need to go there. We need to go through the veil and stand in the spirit. "In the spirit" means the other side of the veil, not this side of the veil. *"What then if you should see the Son of Man ascend where He was before? It is the Spirit who gives life; the flesh profits nothing. The words that I speak to you are spirit, and they are life*" (John 6:62-63 NKJV). We need to get this because the triggers of our old pathways will continue to preside over us. These pathways will dictate to us unless we reinforce the new pathways of thinking over and over. We have got to overlay the limited understanding of the past that we learned and thought was true: "*No man puts a piece of new cloth onto an old garment, for that which is put on to fill it up takes from the garment, and the tear is made worse*" (Matthew 9:16).

It was true in its day but our understanding of the truth of yesterday does not fit today, and today's truth does not fit into yesterday's understanding.

In the early 1900's they had no idea of television, cell phones or computers. If we were to take today's world and try and fit it into the early 1900's, it would not work. In the same way you cannot take the early 1900's understanding and try to make our day conform to that day. Yet we often try and do that. *Of the tribe of Issachar, men who understood the times, with knowledge of what Israel should do, two hundred chiefs; and all their relatives were at their command*" (1 Chronicles 12:32 AMP). "*For my thoughts are not your thoughts, neither are your ways my ways, says the LORD. For as the heavens are higher than the earth, so are my ways higher than your ways, and my thoughts than your thoughts*" (Isaiah 55:8-9 KJV).

We hold on to the past because we are not yoked to His unknowable awesomeness, "*God is so great, greater than we can understand*" (Job 36:26 EXB). We are yoked to what we have known. What we have known is insufficient for what is coming. So we have got to be willing to let go of what we have known to go into the unknown, as YHVH leads us, beyond even our understanding. No doctrine or understanding of the past will be relevant or able to explain what is coming. as it is so beyond what we have known.

If you have no understanding or knowledge of some of this, that does not mean it is wrong. It just means you do not have the understanding yet to measure it according to your current belief system. The only way to come to such an understanding is to be willing to let go of your wrong belief system and allow Him to lead you. Remember the Word says *"Eye has not seen, nor ear heard, neither have entered into the heart of man, the things which God has prepared for them that love him"*(1 Corinthians 2:9).

A scriptural example of this is Abraham's faith walk: *"By faith, Abraham, when he was called [by God], obeyed by going to a place which he was to receive as an inheritance; and he went, not knowing where he was going"* (Hebrews 11:8 AMP).

Can you imagine the conversation?

"Hi, Honey, we are leaving all we have known today and we are going to a new place."

…"Where is that, darling?"

"Not sure honey"

"How long is it going to take to get there?"

"Not sure honey"

"How do you know whereabouts this place is?"

"The Lord said He will show me!"

Can you imagine how that would go down today within your marriage?

The earthly pattern does not understand the things of heaven. Similar to the Essenes (who we know because of the writings of Josephus and the Dead Sea Scrolls) who took themselves away from the Hebrew social structure of the time to go after the "city of YHVH". What Abraham was looking for was only found by supernatural revelation of YHVH, *"And the LORD said unto Abram, after Lot was separated from him, "Lift up now your eyes, and look from the place where you are northward, and southward, and eastward, and westward: For all the land which you see, to you will I give it, and to your descendants forever. And I will make your descendants as the dust of the earth: so that if a man can number the dust of the earth, then shall your descendants also be numbered. Arise, walk through the land in the length of it and in the breadth of it; for I will give it unto you"* (Genesis 13:14-17 AMP).

YHVH is positioning us to become oracles

When YHVH comes, He feeds us solid food. The big problem is we do not really believe we can be an oracle of God to bring the revelation of YHVH as a priest, from a kingly position, in fire, framing what has never been framed before in our day. We rely too much on past belief systems.

"For when for the time you ought to be teachers, you have need that one teach you again which be the first principle of the oracles of God; and are become such as have need of milk, and not of solid food. For every one that uses milk is unskillful in the word of righteousness: for he is a babe. But solid food belongs to them that are of full age, even those who by reason of use have their senses exercised to discern both good and evil" (Hebrew 5:12-14).

Hebrew culture understood that the Rabbis were the mouthpiece or the oracles of YHVH to them. The people accepted that these Rabbis could change their recorded processes and bring something new that would be absorbed and assimilated into their community because they considered it to have come out from heaven, even though they had not heard it before. Yeshua said, *"For where your treasure is, there your heart will be also. The light of the body is the eye: if, therefore, your eye be sound* (if you have a generous or single minded heart attitude[16]) *"your whole body shall be full of light"* (Matthew 6:21-2). He was talking about *Terumah,* and what they believed about *Terumah*[17]. Because we do not understand the culture and often don't read the original manuscript, we do not always understand what is going on. We read an interpretation of someone else's belief system or we are taught outside of the culture it was delivered into.

We need to understand that YHVH is positioning us to become oracles. When we speak, our voice goes beyond the atmosphere of the earth. It is often described in science as *the Butterfly Effect.* It is described as this, where there is a little puff of air here but a million miles away it creates a tornado. There

[16] For further insight into this biblical idiom see: http://www.biblicalhebrew.com/nt/goodeye.htm

[17] Terumah means contribution, gift or free will offering, *"And the LORD spoke unto Moses, saying, Speak unto the children of Israel, that they bring me an offering: of every man that gives it willingly with his heart you shall take my offering"* (Exodus 25:1-2). The Lord asked for help from everyone whose heart moved them to provide gifts from the heart. (Hebrew4Christians.com)

is life in our breath because our breath should also carry the words of life, so when you breathe out, it carries the revelation to frame that which has not been seen. The reason we breathe is to frame what YHVH is calling into being. We should live to breathe, not simply breathe to live. Because of this, what seems like a little "Yes" spoken right here, becomes a tornado of glory out there. As the Bible says, *"And many people shall go and say, Come, and let us go up to the mountain of the LORD, to the house of the God of Jacob; and he will teach us of his ways, and we will walk in his paths: for out of Zion shall go forth the law, and the word of the LORD from Jerusalem"* (Isaiah 2:3). When you go into Zion, you go into the house of the government of His presence not found in the earth.

When we begin to engage with YHVH and we stand in the heavens, the Bible says, *"I will put my law in their inward parts, and write it in their hearts; and will be their God, and they shall be my people"* (Jeremiah 31:33). It also says that we would not need the sun and the moon for light because He will be our light. *"The sun shall be no more your light by day; neither for brightness shall the moon give light unto you: but the LORD shall be unto you an everlasting light, and your God your glory"* (Isaiah 60:19). When we stand as an oracle, the light of the glory of the countenance of YHVH is going to shine around and through you and men will not understand by the reasoning's of their mind. We will not understand the revelation that YHVH is bringing into the earth by the reasoning's of our understanding because it will go too far beyond that. The irrefutable evidence of the glory of YHVH in the land of the living will testify to what is happening, even though we do not understand it through our current belief systems.

YHVH is bringing things that we have not seen before

YHVH is bringing into creation things that we have not seen before. Many of those who have been captured by YHVH and operating out of the Melchizedek priesthood have been crying out for more than they currently have, where they have laboured in the spirit for revelation of their future to come to the earth and be seen in creation. They know what it means to stand in the East Gate; I describe it as, "the way of the mysteries of YHVH" which is where the Father's Son is going to be revealed from. "*Then he (the angel) led me to the gate, the gate that faces toward the east. And behold, the glory and brilliance of the God of Israel was coming from the way of the east; and His voice was like the sound of many waters, and the earth shone with His glory*" (Ezekiel 43:1-2 AMP). YHVH is revealing Himself, from the East Gate. People of every nation, culture and tongue are going to bear witness to this because He has always had a remnant. It is going to happen because their voice is coming up from the scrolls within them that YHVH has written and spoken over them as a testimony from the beginning.

When this begins to happen, there is going to come a unity in the beloved. It is not going to be about any individual person or senior leader or 'who's-who' in the Church, because we are all going to be called sons. We will all have a responsibility. This is not about one person doing it all. This is about responsibility for landing what YHVH wants in the earth today, revealed by us all, where every eye will see, all at the same time.

The apostolic, governmental move that has been on the face of the earth has been busy but not always effective. Some have done a good job but others have built hierarchical structures for themselves. I believe that YHVH is inviting the Apostolic Government to embrace the maturity of son-ship, to step into the Melchizedek order as sons, forsaking the earthly image of position. The Melchizedek order functions in heaven, engages in heaven, walks in heaven, and legislates from heaven to the earth. Under the Melchizedek Government, everyone is responsible to come into full maturity, to bear an image of heaven on the earth.

Brief history of the five-fold offices

Briefly looking at some recent church history will hopefully be helpful for you. In the 1950s, YHVH began to overshadow the earth with an increased expression of *Evangelism* or the mandate of the evangelist, where hundreds and thousands of people began to get saved in tent crusades etc. The poor evangelists suddenly realised that there were a lot of needs in all of these people getting saved because they all had brokenness and needed to be pastored.

So, around the 1960s, YHVH began to release and overshadow the earth with the *Pastoral* mandate. Due to this, people began to be cared for. However, the pastors began to get overworked because they were often dealing with the same thing with lots of people every week on an individual basis. That seems to be what pastors do. They are willing to go from person to person dealing with the same things all the time. Often, this is because people are not mature enough to deal with their own brokenness. That is okay if you remain immature, but perhaps there is a problem if you are fifty years old and still needing counseling. As scripture says! *"Therefore, leaving the basic teaching of the Messiah, let us move on toward maturity… But even though we speak like this, loved ones, concerning you, we are convinced of better things – things coming with salvation… so you will not be sluggish but imitators of those inheriting the promises through trust and perseverance…* And so after waiting patiently, Abraham reached the promise" (Hebrews 6:1, 9, 12, 15 TLV).

Around the 1970s, YHVH released another overlay and calling this was the *Teacher.* They brought instruction to help the process, and teach groups rather than individuals, which could then be shepherded by the pastor and engaged by the evangelist. Remember, all this process is still man on earth reaching into heaven to try and find an answer.

Around the 1980s, after the teacher's mantle had been unlocked for several years, unusual things started happening where people started to have spiritual experiences and the awareness and knowledge of the gifts of the Holy Spirit began to be released. The office and the overlay of the prophet began to encompass the face of the earth. The prophetic realm began to be released and revelation started to land on the earth from heaven. Heaven was being uncovered in a mystical way. Unfortunately, I believe that, over time, this became an institution and lost its way. Suddenly, almost everybody wanted to be a prophet and prophecy. It became very messy. This became the launching pad for the overlay and office of the Apostle to bring divine order into the chaos that now seemed to be everywhere.

The prophetic movement needed order in it so YHVH began to overlay the earth with the *Apostolic.* I noticed that many who had been prophets suddenly became apostles (except for those who understood their role, function and position). This apostolic mandate then became a network of churches or a ministry instead of a body of matured believers. In my opinion, this missed what it was designed for. Therefore, YHVH had to release the Melchizedek order into creation to shift the responsibility to maturity of sonship and not just in a calling that only has an earthly office.

"And he gave some, apostles; and some, prophets; and some, evangelists; and some, pastors and teachers; For the perfecting of the saints, for the work of the ministry, for the edifying of the body of Christ: ***Until*** *we all come in the unity of the faith, and of the knowledge of the Son of God, unto a perfect man, unto the measure of the stature of the fullness of Christ"* (Ephesians 4:11-13).

The word "until" in this scripture signifies that the five-fold ministry is not going to exist any longer when the maturing or perfecting of the beloved is complete. Some of us seemed to take the whiteout/tippex pen and rub that word out of our reading of the Bible because we wanted to have a title in front of our name. YHVH is now releasing that which is perfect into the earth as sons rise into the Order of Melchizedek to bring the Lord's dominion beyond the current church system or network to the whole earth and then into creation. This will function from heaven to earth, not from earth to heaven.

Serving another mountain

Some have built mountains on the earth with someone at the top who are often called apostles. Everyone who wants to be a part of this mountain must move under the government of this mountain to serve it. They may not realise that the person that sits at the top of the mountain will have access to every realm that you have an anointing in through you serving them. You have empowered them to do their job better by them having access to what you have.

When you pay to belong to that 'network', you might not realise that, through your trading into that mountain, the anointing in *your* life is feeding into that mountain and all who have influence in the top positions have complete access to what you have.

It is actually called 'trading' which in the end leads to something called 'covering'. When this is abused, it can become one of the biggest forms of control exercised over the body of Christ today.

In the mountain or network that was built, the apostle or senior leader would bring the vision because we "must have a vision". Some of us wanted to know what to do because we just want to serve. What we were really asking for was a king to rule over us, to tell us what to do, mostly because we did not want to take responsibility for our own actions.

As our desire was to do the will of YHVH, we served the vision willingly. People serve in this way, many unwittingly, not knowing what is happening. As a result, the vision can swerve off track, by becoming task orientated or programme focused and financially driven. "We have a budget that must be met" and this shifts from relationship to 'things I need to do'. We now get into the formula. I hear the question 'What am I doing' coming out of the mouths.

After so many cycles of this happening for me personally, and after serving in one church for 24 years, I started saying, "What am I doing?". This is the same thing I am hearing worldwide coming out of the mouths of some senior leaders while ministering at conferences; "What am I doing, why am I here, there has got to be more".

YHVH is starting to move differently in our day. There is a shift taking place because we have been serving in this way and coming into this structure for so long. All we know is to serve the vision and structure in this way. The young people today are asking, "What is the vision. If I could just get hold of the vision, it will all be okay". I believe much of this is happening because of what we have sown. This will only change when we start to teach them to engage and take responsibility for their own lives with YHVH and become what YHVH is looking for – a mature mandated son on earth functioning out of heaven.

What is YHVH asking you to do?

The question to really ask is, "What is YHVH asking *me* to do? What is your mandate? What is the Father asking *you* to do in the earth for Him so that you can bring the image of heaven to the earth, called being *"under the shadow of the Almighty"* (Psalm 91:1). He is shifting from the local body to the corporate Son. This is the evidence of the Melchizedek Order beginning to function, with all of us walking together to work out His plan here but individually taking responsible to bear the image we have been shown.

What the Father is now doing is bringing something completely different. It is now no longer about the earth reaching up to or pulling stuff out of heaven or pressing into heaven – that is the old system. It is about heaven reaching into earth and from there being administrated into the earth.

YHVH is now releasing a 'Blueprint' from heaven. If you try to draw it, it looks like squiggles all over a whiteboard. There is no recognizable pattern to get a vision from because it is 'all-in-all' and just a shadow on a flat surface of a multi dimensional pattern. If you look, you can see there is something really interesting happening. This image on the surface comes from a light shining down from above, forming a flat line down here on the earth. This is called a shadow.

What I believe YHVH is saying now is, "Where will you position yourself to take responsibility to build *that* piece in My shadow and image, taken from the pattern of the shadow from heaven, that you can now see and that has been revealed to you as your part? Where are you positioning yourself in My shadow to build *this particular* piece? Where is someone else positioning themselves in My shadow to build *their* piece?" It is now about all of us building to the extent of the vision that YHVH wants for us individually and out of maturity to establish His house and blue print. Where we take responsibility for our own actions, our own resources and whatever is necessary. When everyone stands in their place we will be able to turn to those on either side and say "Hey, what can we do to help you fulfill that? What is YHVH saying to you?" This will bring maturity through you being responsible for your own actions. No longer is the body there to meet your need but to serve the blueprint from heaven that YHVH is revealing in a corporate way. There was a study conducted in America recently where ten thousand church-going people were interviewed. There was one common question that was asked of every single one of those people: "Why do you think the church is here?" Apparently ninety-three percent of them said, "To meet my needs". I think this is completely immature.

Your maturity will be measured by your service

YHVH is asking you to come into an order that goes beyond the five-fold order we currently have, into a Kingly order that bears an image on earth of 'as it is in heaven.' It is called the Melchizedek

order. This image means responsibility. You are responsible for where you serve. Your service must start in heaven. The measure of your maturity is going to be measured by your service, not by what you do or have done on the earth. No longer are you just able to come into a meeting or a conference and suck out of the atmosphere and anointing. If you do this, it means you have been too lazy during the week to form your own connection with YHVH. No longer can we draw on the atmosphere to make us feel better because we have not been engaging with YHVH. I believe there are two reasons we do not engage with YHVH. We say "I can't", but it is either because you do not want to and are lazy or because you have never been shown how to.

YHVH is looking for maturity within His bod, so that we will bear an image on the earth of 'as it is in heaven.' Do you realise that one of the reasons that YHVH has not visited the earth in the way some of us want Him to is because we do not bear an image that looks like Him in heaven on earth.

YHVH is giving and releasing a new pattern. Your function in heaven is about becoming a mature son, functioning as a king and a priest. You become the one that engages and become the revelation of the pattern He has revealed. Then you bring the revelation of the fullness of what you are supposed to be doing to the earth from your life with Him in heaven.

When you engage within the Melchizedek order as king and priest, it brings rulership and releases legislation of what has being seen and experienced in heaven into the earth. When it is administered from heaven, you will then become the mouthpiece (the oracle) which frames what has been witnessed in heaven. True government is brought to it through the legislator who becomes the fire while the oracle becomes the voice. You frame your functioning on the earth as legislator and oracle by your connection in the Spirit with your kingly and priestly roles in heaven.

Have you wondered how this fits into the current church model? It does not. It is amazing how, even though the current model and system is in many ways not functioning towards maturity, we will still try and fit into the current functional models and have them as an add-on to what is operating instead of a complete change.

YHVH wants us to bear the image of heaven

We have to realise that YHVH now wants a different image. He is calling to His sons to "come up here". It is only out of our function in heaven that the earth is going to bear the reflection and image of heaven. To help understand this concept, if I was to ask a small woman to stand next to me and we stood in the light and I looked at my shadow and then looked at her shadow, which would be a bit smaller and thinner than mine, I could not say that her shadow is my shadow or even looks like my shadow.

Why do we expect YHVH to acknowledge us when we

do not bear the shadow of what He wants us to bear on the earth? If we want YHVH to come into our house we need to look like heaven. Why do we cry out all the time for Him to come in if we do not even bear the external image that we are supposed to look like? We have not fitted into what He wants but have fitted into what a man wants. *"In whom all the building fitly framed together grows unto a holy temple in the Lord: In whom you also are built together for a habitation of God through the Spirit"* (Ephesians 2:21-22).

Here is another thing that also affects the image of YHVH here in creation. The human heart emanates radiation of what you are thinking about and forms visible patterns around you. Whatever is in your heart is going to be seen as an image around your life. It will be seen by everyone, the darkness as well as the light. *"Search me, O God, and know my heart; test my thoughts. Point out anything you find in me that makes you sad, and lead me along the path of everlasting life."* (Psalm 139:23-24 TLB). *"Guard your heart diligently, for from it flow the springs of life" (*Proverbs 4:23 TLV) People want to know if the devil can read your thoughts. Well, in my opinion, yes he can, because your thoughts are seen by the spirit realm as moving images around you. That is why Yeshua spoke so much about the heart. As human beings, we think we are amazing because we can see in seven colours; red, orange, yellow, green, blue, indigo, and violet. If we take those seven colours and put them on seven piano keys, they would only extend across the span of my hand. But if I could add every other part of the electromagnetic spectrum known to man such as ultra-violet, microwave, infra-red etc, and put them on the same keyboard, that keyboard would physically reach from here to the moon.

Your heart radiates all around your life – whatever is in you comes out and is seen. Whatever image you are bearing dictates what is going to sit over your life. When you are in the spirit, all of the radiation and electromagnetic spectrum is opened up. There is no secret when you are in the spirit because everything is seen. That is why love can cover a multitude of sins because you see it all. You can walk around a person and look at them and tell them everything about their life, what has happened and what they have done because it is all seen. I have known people to fast for three weeks and try not to sin before coming to a meeting, thinking that then I will not see their stuff. They are worried that I will expose it. I need you to know I can see beyond your three weeks. And I can still look at you and say that I love you. That includes all of your mess-ups and all the little things you have got hidden away in your heart. Even still they radiate an image that is born on the outside of your body that the spirit-world can see.

True repentance rewrites our image

There is something that I find really fascinating: true repentance rewrites the image. It rewrites the image and makes it something completely different. Then the spirit world sees that as well. So the more you are involved in repenting and engaging YHVH the more you come into deeper and deeper relationship with Him. Coming into a depth of relationship with the presence of the Father brings a greater measure of redemption and, the greater that is, the more you will begin to look like Christ.

That is why the devil comes to you and says, "Give me a man that I might fight with" (1 Samuel 17:8). He accuses you and wants you to say, "Oh, no, I have not sinned." But the Bible tells us to agree with our adversary quickly (Matthew 5:25). Why? Repent and get the accusations against you judged so they have no power over you. Judge your house. *"If you will walk in my ways, and if you will keep my charge, then you shall also judge my house, and shall also keep my courts, and I will give you places to walk among these that stand here"* (Zechariah 3:7). The Bible says, *"The standard you use in judging is the standard by which you will be judged"* (Matthew 7:2 NLT). So we must judge ourselves first. (See the chapter: *Judge Your House;* MP3 teaching: *The Mobile Court* and *The Courtroom of God* in Realms of the Kingdom Volume 1).

This becomes very important for us, because YHVH is doing something very different on the earth today than what He has done in the past. In December 2012, I believe that the Melchizedek government began superseding the apostolic government on the earth. The Melchizedek order is about a heavenly kingly/priestly order, not about an earthly order. There is nothing wrong with being an apostle. Praise the Lord for your labour – the apostles have done amazing work carrying the responsibility of what YHVH has been doing in their day but their day ended to make way for this new order and government in creation. I believe the cloud of YHVH is moving and, as sons, we must walk within it and not get stuck in an old camp or form of functioning. It is about being in His world and His Kingdom, facilitating and understanding legislation from the realm of heaven and being in that world with the Father. It is, also, about understanding our role as a king and priest of YHVH and being able to become the oracle or mouthpiece of YHVH in the earth today. It is different from what we have been used to but, just because it is different, does not mean it is wrong

This has got nothing to do with what has been described as the sovereignty of YHVH, though it has got to do with desire. In the 1960s, 70s, 80s, and 90s it was about sovereignty. But the church was never brought to maturity about desire. The Word says, *"… whatever things you desire, when you pray, believe that you will receive them, and you shall have them"* (Mark 11:24). Desire is a gate that opens up the realm of heaven to every believer. Desire becomes an anchor and a doorway of entry into the world of the Father and, as you delight yourself in Him, YHVH grants you the desires of your heart (Psalm 37:4).

The old will fight the new

Holy Spirit is doing some weird stuff, really weird stuff and I love it. I am looking forward to the day where we can gather together from Scotland, Ireland, Wales, Africa, America, Canada, New Zealand, Australia, Singapore and the four corners of the earth and meet in heaven before the Father. The cloud of YHVH is moving. Do not get stuck in on old camp when the cloud of the Lord lead's off and moves. History has shown us that the old order is going to fight against the new when the new starts to raise its head above that which has been established. This has been an historical pattern which may continue. Unless there is a joining to the image of where that cloud is moving, you will fight against it.

Those who want to move with the cloud will often be shocked by those who want to stay stuck in the past. There is, as yet, little understanding or knowledge of what this new order looks like as no one has been this way before. That is why you have got to yoke yourself to the mystery of the dark cloud of His presence until the mystery gets unlocked and becomes normal life *"I will give you treasures of darkness and hidden riches of secret places so you may know that I am Adonai the God of Israel who calls you by your name"* (Isaiah 45:3 TLV). Only then will you understand life from a completely different perspective and then YHVH will be able to do what He wants to do inside our lives by the power of Holy Spirit. *"Not by might, nor by power, but by my spirit, says the LORD of hosts"* (Zechariah 4:6).

When YHVH breathes into the earth something completely new, we try and figure it out with our current beliefs and paradigms. We try and reason it out to get an understanding of it. The problem is that our understanding is too small to fit all that is new into what we currently believe and we need new structures of belief systems to land what YHVH is doing today. We do not understand it so we often start resisting it because it does not fit into our current belief system. It is because your current belief system will be challenged and often does not want to change. We have got to be open to change which can be the hardest thing for us to do.

We have got to be willing to yoke ourselves to Him so that He draws us along into the mystery, even if we do not understand it. Did you know we do not have to understand everything YHVH says and does? We have just got to be willing to move with the cloud as He leads.

Dream about where others go

Joshua is one person I am still fascinated by in the Bible. I have drunk his wine, and I have spent time with him, trying to engage what he did. The Bible says that Moses went into the tabernacle and Joshua came in with him. Then when it came time for them to go out, it says that Moses went out but Joshua stayed in and there is no record of Joshua ever coming out.

"As Moses went into the tent, the pillar of cloud would come down and stay at the entrance, while the LORD spoke with Moses… And the LORD spoke unto Moses face to face, as a man speaks to his friend. And he turned again into the camp: but his servant Joshua, the son of Nun, a young man, departed not out of the tabernacle" (Exodus 33:9, 11).

Joshua and Caleb, from scripture, appear to have been good friends. What Joshua did by staying in the tent of The Lord's presence (Exodus 33:11) so changed him that it would have had a definite impact on Caleb because the Word says he had a different spirit (Numbers 14:24). I have no doubt that they would have had some very deep discussions within their friendship and would have dreamed together of their future. Dreaming about where others are will change where we currently are, especially with those that are much further down the line than we are. Dreaming is a faith arena activity that will help bring us into what is beyond today and help us reach into the future. That is why I believe Caleb could go to Joshua and asked for his mountain, *"Today I am eighty-five years old. I am as strong now as I was when Moses sent me on that journey, and I can still travel and fight as well as I could then. So give me the hill country that the LORD promised me. You will remember that, as scouts, we found the descendants of Anak living there in great, walled towns. But, if the LORD is with me, I will drive them out of the land, just as the LORD said"* (Joshua 14:10-12).

Why did Caleb want the mountain? That was where the men of renown lived, the place closer to YHVH and the ruling seats. We are called to rule and reign as the head and not the tail (Deuteronomy 28:13). It is going to come through maturity and repositioning as a mature son. It is going to come to sons who have learnt how to function as kings and priests. It is not just going to come out of the ordination of an office of the five-fold ministry on the earth. It is going to come out of maturity, function and relationship with the Father in heaven.

It will come through being yoked to Christ (Matthew 11:30) and being yoked to the revelation of the knowledge of YHVH, and to what He is doing in the land of the living in this day, reaching into the future. It is not going to come through being yoked to yesterday's revelation, knowledge or doctrine. *"That the God of our Lord Jesus Christ, the Father of glory, may give unto you the spirit of wisdom and revelation in the knowledge of him: The eyes of your understanding being enlightened; that you may know what is the hope of his calling, and what is the riches of the glory of his inheritance in the saints, And what is the exceeding greatness of his power toward us who believe, according to the working of his mighty power, Which he performed in Christ, when he raised him from the dead, and set him at his own right hand in the heavenly places"* (Ephesians 1:17-20).

Doing some new things

YHVH is doing new things. He really is. In the 1970s, there were only a handful of people that would go in and understand being in the councils of YHVH, legislating and holding court. There are a lot more today, coming out from being hidden because it is about the individuals maturing and carrying a pattern from heaven to the earth in a corporate body called the Sons of YHVH.

This thing is important for us, particularly with regards to what is coming over the next ten years. I have been into the year 2057 and we are still here. Sorry for all the rapture theorists. It is different to how it is now but you just need to know we are still here. I grew up in the 1980s, reading books that said the earth was going to finish before the year 1989. Then it was the year 1999, then 2000, then 2006, oops sorry, 2010, oops sorry, 2016, I suppose sometime they may be right if you believe that stuff and are caught up in it. I am pleased to note that we are now well past all these dates. Remember YHVH is looking for a mature body of Sons who know Him and function from within His realm.

Something of interest; when YHVH made Adam he was made him out of the fingerprint of creation, the dust of the earth. There is an imprint and a fingerprint in everything that has been created. All of creation has been designed to respond to man. When we stand in who we are in the Father and, from that position, legislate as a king and priest into all that the father has made.

I was with a group of young people a while ago, sitting at a table with them, discussing some of these things. Some of them were skeptical and I love it when YHVH puts you in a position to challenge people. I told them that there were two major events that were going to happen during the follow year. One was a great, big meteorite that would come through our planetary system and miss the earth by a very small distance and that would not be seen by the astronomers until it went past. Another was, also, going to be a meteorite that would land in a lake of water that would not cause any damage in Russia. I said to the people sitting there, "It is going to hit land, but it will come down in a lake of water. It is not going to achieve the original intent."

That meteor did come through and crashed into a fresh water lake in a remote area of Russia with very little damage. So it was a sign to them. People, we have the capacity to start to direct the affairs of our species if we mature and can work with the Father to become a king and priest and administrate into the affairs of men and affect outcomes.

Creation responds to your DNA when positioned in YHVH

Every created thing has a record that responds to the DNA of the sons of YHVH when we position ourselves in heaven in the Father, *"That they all may be one; as you, Father, are in me, and I in you, that they also may be one in us: that the world may believe that you have sent me"* (John 17:21). All of creation is crying out for governmental legislation to sit over it so it can come back into the light and the glory of the sons of God. Creation desires you to hold your position and come into who you are supposed to be. *"For the earnest expectation of the creation waits for the manifestation of the sons of God"* (Romans 8:19). It is about being in the spirit. *"I (John) was in the spirit on the Lord's day"* (Revelation 1:10) 'In the spirit' means being beyond the veil. It means not praying this side of the veil (outside) but moving through the veil into the Father's world and, from there, moving into the testimony of Christ in the Father. It is about being a witness in heaven of what the Father is doing. Then, out of being a witness, it means having others that stand and witness with us to legislate as a witness into creation, framing His will around us.

I hope this chapter has challenged and unhinged you from some restrictions. No one said it would be easy but it will be possible.

Let's finish with a scripture, *"Beloved, now we are the sons of God, and it doth not yet appear what we shall be; but we know that, when He shall appear, we shall be like Him; for we shall see Him as He is"* (1 John 3:2 KJ21).

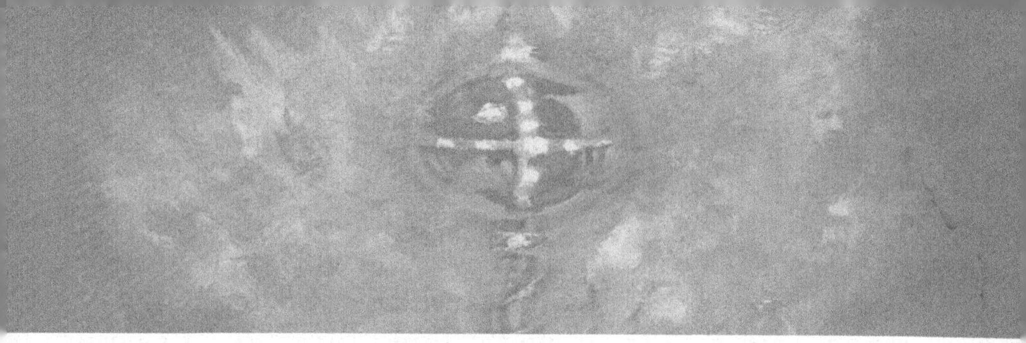

Chapter 10
Legislator and Oracle

I really want to honour the work that Melchizedek has done in working with the Father to bring us to a point where we can begin to express the fullness of YHVH.

Four faces of YHVH and Melchizedek

YHVH expresses Himself through the four faces of a Lion, an Ox, an Eagle and a Man. I believe that sitting within each of these four faces are also the expression of the four faces of Melchizedek; and we must learn how to functionally express these from within the framework of our union in Him into the earth and then into all of creation. They are the King, the Priest, the Oracle and the Legislator.

Legislator and Oracle – earthly shadows

The King and Priest are heavenly offices (the way we actually function out of in heaven), that empower a physically connected function of the Oracle and Legislator. This is to operate the framework of the Oracle and Legislator which provides the shadow in this realm that has the image of the heavenly offices, and provides a resting place for the government of those heavenly offices to function from, so that what is in heaven can rest within creation. Remember, heaven will not sit and rest into anything that does not look like itself. Only what it recognises as its own will it engage with.

In heaven we have the two faces of the King and the Priest that we represent on earth. The function of these two in heaven is to form an arc which opens up a window; through them a reflection can then be seen that rests on the earth. The Priest and King are going to bear a reflection on the earth but all of this will not come into full measure until it has the earthly offices of the Oracle and the Legislator standing with it. As we shall see, the Oracle and the Legislator are two strands of a cord. This whole dynamic is very important for us because the earth needs to have a container to be able to retain what YHVH is revealing to us within creation and you and I are the vessel of the expression of this.

Yeshua was confirmed and authorised at His transfiguration

Yeshua did some amazing things, so you had better believe we are also going to be doing some amazing things. I think one of the weirdest things that Yeshua ever did and had happen to Him was His transfiguration. I do not know about you, but I want transfiguration!

Yeshua went through His early life learning how to become a vessel for the impossible. At His water baptism, the Father said, *"This is my beloved Son, in whom I am well pleased"* (Matthew 3:17). This is the Father's affirmation of His Person. At His transfiguration, the Father said, *"This is My Son, whom I love; with Him I am well pleased. Listen to Him!"* (Matthew 17:5). This is no longer just affirming His Person as a Son, we are now told to listen to Him, which is saying something very different. It is a confirmation and an establishing of position and an authorisation for action. We have no scriptural record of the Father authorising Yeshua's position for action before He was transfigured.

As Yeshua was the firstborn of many (Colossians 1:15), you had better believe that transfiguration is going to happen on the face of the earth to them that come to full maturity, because through Him we are *"filled with all the fullness of God"* (Ephesians 3:19). One of the biggest frustrations for me, is that many people have unwittingly made a covenant with death by completely limiting themselves and saying, "Only one day, when I die, will I see heaven, or will I understand the fullness of God." If you do this it makes death your saviour and rescuer, because you believe only death will produce the knowledge of YHVH for you.

The Oracle

"The words of a king are like a message from God [oracle], so his decisions should be fair [he should not betray justice with his mouth]" (Proverbs 16:10 EXB).

The office of the oracle under the Order of Melchizedek has nothing to do with the ordination and the office of the prophet in the fivefold ministry. The realm of the ordination of the Melchizedek Oracle is about having the ability to legislate on earth the fullness of YHVH in order to see the glory of heaven rest on the earth.

Yeshua said, "*The words I speak are spirit and are life*" (John 6:63). The Word says, *"My word… always produces fruit. It will accomplish all I want it to, and it will prosper everywhere I send it"* (Isaiah 55:1). That sounds to me a bit more powerful than just prophesying over someone. The problem is we get carried away. We often do not realize that we are accountable for every single word that has come out of our mouth in prophecy. We are accountable for the discipleship of that word, watching over that word, brooding over the word and discipling people into the fullness of the word we have given them. Most of what we call 'prophecy' is actually not. There is a difference between speaking a word of knowledge about something to reveal the future for someone and being an oracle. All of us can prophesy, but not all of us can say, "every word I say brings forth fruit from the earth," (as Yeshua talks about in John 15:2).

"And Balaam said to Balak, "Look, I have come to you! Now, have I any power at all to say anything? The word that God puts in my mouth, that I must speak" (Numbers 22:38 NKJV).

And Balaam raised his eyes, and saw Israel encamped according to their tribes; and the Spirit of God came upon him. Then he took up his oracle and said: "The utterance of Balaam the son of Beor, The utterance of the man whose eyes are opened, The utterance of him who hears the words of God, Who sees the vision of the Almighty..." (Numbers 24: 2-4 NKJV).

The office of the Oracle completely exposes the footstool of the government of heaven. YHVH will sit into it because the earth has born the reflection of as it is in heaven. This heavenly reflection needs a footstool for kingship and priesthood to be fully revealed on the earth. This happens when the words of creation are spoken through the office of the oracle. YHVH is looking in us for the ability to materialise matter out of creative light.

In December 2012 I believe that an age concluded because many seer visionaries only saw into the future until then. The Bible reaches beyond that point but only in visionary form, it does not tell us literal details about everything that is going to happen. *"No one knows the day or hour when these things will happen"* (Matthew 24:36). This is because YHVH expects a 'voice' to co-write history. YHVH is looking for the revealing of something completely different to anything the human race has ever seen or will ever have the ability to perceive. *"If someone says to this mountain, 'Be taken up and thrown into the sea,' and does not doubt in his heart but trusts that what he says is happening, so shall it be for him"* (Mark 11:23 TLV). YHVH is looking for a *mouthpiece* that is going to materialise the substance of His will into being. *"For I will give you words and wisdom that none of your adversaries will be able to resist or contradict"* (Luke 21:15).

Everything for a Hebrew is circular because the beginning must meet the end. There is a point called the 'matrix' which can be called the event horizon, where the beginning and the end come together. It is the opening doorway between the beginning and the end. When you live in this matrix of the beginning and the end you can see the end of a matter and see its beginning. With every choice you make you can see the fruit of it at the end. So, you make right choices because you can see 'the end' of it. This is priesthood. This is the operation of the function of what YHVH wants on the face of the earth. He does not want someone to just have a ministry. So, on 20th December 2012, I believe that a complete new dispensational period began in the history of mankind. Things are going to be occurring in this time that no one has ever seen happen. YHVH is unlocking the secrets of heaven and He is looking for a mouthpiece, an oracle, who has seen the revelation of the glory of YHVH and has learnt about rulership as a priest and king in heaven. *"…The one who has My word should speak it with unshakable faith. For what is straw worth, when compared to grain? Does not My word burn like fire? Does it not shatter rock like a strong hammer?"* (Jeremiah 23:28-29 VOICE). He wants a mouthpiece that can begin to dictate to the earth what is going to happen. YHVH is looking for you to take dominion over the earth in the office of the oracle *"And the LORD shall make you the head, and not the tail; and you shall be above only, and you shall not be beneath; if that you hearken unto the commandments of the LORD your God"* (Deuteronomy 28:13). It is one of the four faces of the legislative governmental order of Melchezidek. It means having the ability to terra-form the face of the earth, to change times and seasons that have been producing death such as drought or flooding, to set precedents, and to set the parameters and boundaries of how things will be, bringing life. *"If my people, who are called by my name, shall humble themselves, and pray, and seek my face, and turn from their wicked ways; then will I hear from heaven, and will forgive their sin, and will heal their land"* (2 Chronicles 7:14). As you can see, it goes a long way beyond prophesying. The Father would come to me and say: "Son, watch your words, because of the *Office*." I would ask, "What do You mean, 'because of the Office'? Do you mean prophet, apostle, teacher, evangelist, pastor? What are You talking about?" Then I began to uncover the truth about the Order of Melchizedek and the maturity, or the responsibility necessary, knowing that what you say may happen. I hope you understand the issue of responsibility here.

Can you imagine having the ability to say to a mountain: "Hey you! Go up in the air and move over there!" (Mark 11:23). I wonder what the army would do if they came to get you and you levitated off the ground, ascended up into the clouds, disappeared, and then materialised again. What if they shot you and the bullets went right through you without harming you because you were a solid space of glory. I believe we are going to hear increased testimony of miracles likes guns aimed at us falling to the floor and melting because the material substance of things around us changed at our word.

Both Elijah and Jeremiah knew about this reality. *"There shall not be dew nor rain these years, but according to my word"* (1 Kings 17:1). Personally I think the King would have laughed at him, In my language something like "*Ha-ha, ha-ha.* Yeah, right mate." Several years later the King was saying: "Go and find that guy!" (1 Kings 18:1-17). Elijah was a forerunner of a reality that YHVH wants to rest on the earth, with responsibility in a greater measure.

Can you imagine what would happen if we did things like this:

"Okay, Father – we need a forest", and you materialise it.

"Oh, we need a new mountain today."

"Oh, right in the middle of Washington? H*mm*... okay. Done." I think you would have the media's attention!

Transposing the equation $E=mc^2$ ($m= E/c^2$) shows you how to produce mass (m) out of the speed of light (c) and energy (E). Everything in this world came out of light, with great energy, which is the Voice that framed it. This office of the oracle is about bringing a completely different framework to contain something that has never been seen before. When I was taken into the year 2057, they were growing plants and building things without physical involvment, materialising matter out of the atomic structure of the universe. I want that! The oracle is about 'the voice', or the ability to understand the framework of what is needed to bring life.

The Bible says that YHVH brought the animals before Adam for him to name them (Genesis 2:20). He did that because Adam was His voice in the territory over which YHVH had given him responsibility. YHVH did not bring a complete animal to Adam to name. I believe YHVH only brought the divine life spark of that animal before Adam. When Adam spoke its name, that brought a framework into being for completing its physical appearance. This is because the name is its mandate, its structure, its formation, its obligation, and its outworking. Can you imagine creating a new animal? What would the evolutionists do about that? That is why evolution is only a theory.

The mouthpiece of the oracle is about understanding the intrinsic framework of the responsibility that YHVH has given to a son to name something and frame it. This involves being able to create the atmosphere and the realm for its substance to materialise in this world.

A galaxy is simply a pulling together of atoms through the observance of Photons of light that are already out there into a framework of visible substance. The air is full of atoms. You cannot see them yet you believe they are there. Quantum physics tells us that the physical material I can see and touch is largely empty space at the atomic level. The word that we are supposed to speak has a creative ability, just as *"…the faith of Abraham. He is the father of us all (as it is written, "I have made you a father of many nations"). He is our father in the sight of God in whom he trusted, who gives life to the dead and calls into existence that which does not exist"* (Romans 4:16-17 TLV). YHVH gives us this through our responsibility as priests as we gaze into the fullness of the revelation around His glory and look into what He wants. That is why Yeshua said, *"The Son can do nothing of himself, but what he sees the Father do"* (John 5:19). He did not say "What He *hears* the Father say." The key is seeing not hearing.

We really need to come to grips with this whole issue of the framework of creation. It involves the ability to materialise matter through observance of light and speaking it into reality, to engage, to bring what YHVH has need of inside this realm. We need to be able to walk up to a tree and change it as Yeshua did *"Jesus answered, "I tell you the truth, if you have faith and do not doubt, you will be able to do what I did to this tree and even more. You will be able to say to this mountain, '·Go, fall [Be lifted up and thrown] into the sea.' And if you have faith, it will ·happen"* (Matthew 21:21 EXB). *"Then the Lord said, "If you have faith like a mustard seed, you could say to this mulberry tree, 'Be uprooted and planted in the sea,' and it would obey you"* (Luke 17:6 TLV). *"For we know that the whole creation groans and travails in pain together until now"* (Romans 8:22). The trees in Eden look a lot different to trees on the earth. Everything here is dying. Everything you can see that holds a colour, but reflects everything else, is actually dying. This framework that YHVH wants us to understand carries the responsibility of creation. It is bringing forth the essence of the life of who the Father is. He wants us to bring the true *yechida* (the flame of life or the spark of YHVH) of the way that He originally made it to be in Eden. This is called terra-forming.

The Legislator

"Let the rivers applaud and the mountains join in joyful song In the presence of the Eternal because He is coming to judge the earth. He is coming, and His judgment will be what is right for the world and just to all people" (Psalm 98:8-9 VOICE).

The Legislator is the governmental force behind any decree that establishes it as though it is already done. This means when you speak, YHVH answers instantaneously.

"Now it was at the time of offering up the evening sacrifice that Elijah the prophet came near and said, "ADONAI, God of Abraham, Isaac and Israel let it be known today that You are God in Israel, that I am Your servant, and that I have done all these things at Your word. Answer me, ADONAI, answer me, so that these people may know that You, ADONAI, are God, and that You have turned their heart back again." Then the fire of ADONAI fell and consumed the burnt offering – and the wood, the stones and the dust – and licked up the water that was in the trench" (1 Kings 18:36-38 TLV).

"Elijah answered the captain, "If I am a man of God, may fire come down from heaven and consume you and your fifty men!" Then fire fell from heaven and consumed the captain and his men" (2 Kings 1:10).

When Elijah called fire down in 2 Kings 1:10 he had already seen it happen in 1 Kings 18:31-38. He was another forerunner that knew some of this because he lived in that world. Think how much assurance Elijah must have had on in 2 Kings 1:10

to call the fire down. You would be freaked out unless you were fully assured that what the Father had shown you was going to happen. Yet some of the church is like a headless chicken today, running around trying to figure out what YHVH is saying instead of seeing what YHVH is doing.

The legislator functions on the earth alongside the oracle. Together these form a two-stranded cord. They are the earthly manifestation of two of the four faces of Melchizedek: king and priest in heaven, legislator and oracle on the earth. The Order of Melchizedek, through the office of legislative government, brings into life the substance, or the life-giving force so that the word can be framed around the outside of it. In other words, the legislator materialises heaven's substance on earth.

When Yeshua was transfigured, something really important went on. The Bible says that Yeshua went up the mountain and something amazing happened when He was transfigured: two people stood beside Him. One was Moses and the other was Elijah, *"And after six days Jesus took Peter, James, and John his brother, and brought them up into a high mountain apart, And was transfigured before them: and his face did shine as the sun, and his clothing was white as the light. And, behold, there appeared unto them Moses and Elijah talking with him* (Matthew 17:1-3). Let us call Moses the legislator and Elijah the oracle. The Bible says a three-fold cord is not easily broken (Ecclesiastes 4:2). The process that Yeshua went through here is important for us. Because of your function as a priest and a king, those other two offices of legislator and oracle stand beside you making the other two offices of the Melchizedek Order[18].

Interestingly, we presently have a two-strand cord of DNA, yet YHVH's strand of DNA is three-corded. I do teachings on this, see Reams of the Kingdom Volume 1, the *DNA of God* chapter and my MP3 teachings on this subject. And the reason ours is supposed to be also three-corded is because there is an agreement: "as it is in heaven". In heaven there is a 'Bench of

[18] The transfiguration is a picture of Jesus being supported by Moses (who brought the Torah) and Elijah (who brought the prophetic word) which are two things that are sometimes ignored in churches today.

Three': Father, Son and Holy Spirit. Those Three are witnessing with those *three* on the earth in order to establish their realm down here, so that this realm can come into the fullness of that where it came from in the first place (1 John 5:7-8). End-time theology talks about the two men, or witnesses, that could not be killed walking around in Jerusalem. The doctrine we have made around that biblical revelation lacks understanding about what stands in the *middle* of those two witnesses preventing them from being killed. *"And I will give power to my two witnesses, and they will prophesy one thousand two hundred and sixty days, clothed in sackcloth. These are the two olive trees and the two lampstands standing before the God of the earth. And if anyone wants to harm them, fire proceeds from their mouth and devours their enemies"* (Revelation 11:3-5 NKJV).

This issue of transfiguration is the key to the Order of Melchizedek manifesting fully on the earth. Transfiguration is the fullness of YHVH's revelation of the four faces of the Order of Melchizedek being fully revealed in a person. It occurs within the framework of the voice of the oracle, and the ability to bring into being, which has the Legislator's governmental force behind it. That is why the Bible says, *"A thousand shall fall at your side, and ten thousand at your right hand; but it shall not come near you"* (Ps 91:7). *"The name of the LORD is a strong tower: the righteous runs into it, and is safe"* (Proverbs 18:10). Only those who have glorified light can pass through glorified light. Darkness [referring to the point of corruption] cannot enter that. *"Now if our gospel remains veiled, it is only veiled from those who are lost and dying, because the evil god of this age has blinded the minds of unbelievers. As a result the light of the good news, the radiant glory of the Anointed – who is the very image of God – cannot shine down on them"* (2 Corinthians 4:3-4 VOICE). That is also why the Bible says that those who are born of God sin not. *"We know that those who are God's children [are born of/begotten by God]"* (three-folded) *"do not ·continue to sin The ·Son of God [the one born of/begotten by God; Jesus] ·keeps them safe [protects them], and the Evil One [the Devil] cannot touch [harm] them"* (1 John 5:18 EXB).

When the prophetic voice of the oracle and the government

of the legislator are brought into order within us, it completes who we are in YHVH. This then releases the truth of who YHVH is in heaven and also releases your testimony about your position within and with the Father. That is how the world is going to know you are a God-Likened one,a look alike, because they are going to see it on you and in you.

Can you imagine how they will respond: "Oh, no, it is them! What are they going to change today?"

Let's get radical "Hmm… we need some land in the middle of the Pacific. Let's make our own living space shall we?" I wonder how that will go down.

A number of movies are prophesying to the church today that there is another world that we can function out of that can create physical mass in this world and creation. The church seems to have left it behind. YHVH wants to release the fullness of His image into creation. When that gets fully released, it is not going to be the way people told you it is going to be because, *"as it is written, Eye has not seen, nor ear heard, neither have entered into the heart of man, the things which God has prepared for them that love him"* (1 Corinthians 2:9). This means you do not know, nor can any doctrine or experience can tell you from the past what it is going to be like.

In one of the encounters I have had, I have seen Him [refer to the teaching on the Dark cloud, see Realms of the Kingdom Volume 1]. His skin is like a mat of diamonds all woven together with all the colours of the rainbow moving underneath, having an iridescent blue shining through, moving with fire, with His face morphing, going: Lion-Ox-Eagle-Man. I can remember saying ,"how come no one told me that this is what You and I are going to look like.

You will have authority over substance (John 2:1-11). Under this Order, YHVH is going to give us authority over physical matter and natural laws on the face of this earth, *"…in the fourth watch of the night Jesus went unto them, walking on the sea"* (Matthew 14:25). It is His desire that we change the framework of creation back to as it was at the beginning. That is when YHVH first thought about creation before the worlds were formed. The first creation command was "Let there be light" (Genesis 1:3). I believe YHVH is bringing into focus, in the body of Christ worldwide today, the awareness that there is far more going on and available to us than we have been told about. There is also far more power and far more responsibility within the stewardship of creation because we have to look after what we fix.

People go to the top of a mountain and declare: "*Shundy, bundy*! Tear that devil down!" But they leave on Monday so, if you come back on Tuesday, it is back there again. You are responsible to take care of what you free. It is called caretaking. YHVH made Adam a caretaker for all of creation, *"And God blessed them, and God said unto them, Be fruitful, and multiply, and fill the earth, and subdue it: and have dominion over the fish of the sea, and over the fowl of the air, and over every living thing that moves upon the earth"* (Genesis 1:28). We think this is just some lowly occupation. No, YHVH's desire is not just for all the earth, it is for all of creation. YHVH's desire was that the earth would be populated with people that could rule in all of creation *"Then the kingdom and the dominion and the greatness of all the kingdoms under the whole heaven will be given to the people of the saints (believers) of the Most High; His kingdom will be an everlasting kingdom, and all the dominions will serve and obey Him"* (Daniel 7:27 AMP).

Some people are so worried about the earth and what is coming. If you look at the earth, you are going to get what is coming to it, if you look into heaven then you will get what is coming from it. You must live within the supply of what you look into not just from it by just pulling on it as we have been taught. The word tells us what is going to happen anyway *"there shall be famines, and pestilences, and earthquakes"* (Matthew 24:7). The Bible says it is going to happen. *"And you shall hear of wars and rumors of wars"* (Matthew 24:6). If your focus is on this then this will be your reward.

The Bible also says: There is a Rock: "*the stone was cut out of the mountain without hands, and… it broke in pieces the (statue made of) iron, the bronze, the clay, the silver, and the gold*" (Daniel 2:45). And to that Kingdom there will be no end. *"And he shall reign over the house of Jacob forever; and of his kingdom there shall be no end*" (Luke 1:33). And "*Of the increase of his government and peace there shall be no end*" (Isaiah 9:7). I would rather have this scripture as my supply than the other. YHVH is going to do it. So get your eyes focused in the right place and you will get that because you will get what you focus on.

I once got in an argument with YHVH. I do not know if you have ever done that. The reason I do is because there are examples in the Bible where men argued with YHVH and YHVH changed His mind, (Exodus 32:11-14). I do this not out of assumption but out of relationship. So, one day I was standing with some of the chancellors in heaven and the presence of the Lord was there. I sometimes ask questions because I want to know but sometimes I get the most horrendous answer.

I said, "Lord, when are You actually going to come in your full manifestation in your sons?"

And He said, "Son, all I need is one."

And I replied, "What are You talking about: 'All you need is one?'"

He repeated: "All I need is one."

I said, "One what?"

He said, "I need one to come into agreement?"

Amazed I asked, "No. Wait a minute. Let me get this right. Are you saying you just need one person to come into agreement for Your full revelation of sonship to be fully revealed on the earth in that one person?"

"Yes!"

I said, "But You asked for a body."

And He said to me, "That is not what you asked Me."

I said. "But it is a body of people that needs to carry this, not just one!"

He said, "That is not what you asked me."

I said, "But, Lord. But, but, but, but…" You know how it kind of degenerates.

Until He says, "But all I need is one to come into agreement. The issue is My grace has rested on the body because there has always been one."

So I started an argument for six months.

"Lord, You said You have got a body of people that are going to be glorified."

"Yes, all I need is one."

"No! You have got a body of people that need to be glorified?"

"Yes, all I need is one."

"No!"

Six months! I gave up in the end because He is true. What He says is totally true.

Later on, I was engaging with Melchizedek and allowing him to teach me. Melchizedek is very wise in stewarding the hidden mysteries and he said to me, "The four faces must shine first, son." Finally, I understood what he meant because YHVH is looking for the full revelation of Himself in us before He is going to come. And until that happens, His grace is sufficient to take us through to where we need to be.

When you shine on earth with Moses and Elijah, (who are the other two cords), *you* also open up an arc to reveal a window in heaven. Therefore, over this function of the two-stranded cord of the Oracle and Legislator, there is always an open heaven. That means there is no hindrance to seeing the glory of YHVH, or what YHVH is doing. This means we are instantaneously looking at His glory on a continual basis all the time.

The reflection of legislator and oracle on earth must bear the full image of king and priest in heaven. The only reason it is going to have a reflection down here is because you have spent the time cultivating it there, because it must be "*on earth as it is in heaven*" (Matthew 6:10 AMP), not "in heaven as it is on earth."

What YHVH is releasing into the world today goes far beyond anything our imagination can ever perceive. *"Of the increase of his government and peace there shall be no end"* (Isaiah 9:7). It is going to be amazing being able to materialise substance out of the web of atoms that form dark matter (which all used to be creative light). But then we will have a responsibility. Whatever you make and create, you are responsible for. That is why Adam was the one who framed the animals with life within their name when he spoke their name because he was to have responsibility over them.

You and I are going to see weird things in the near future. Unusual things are going to start to happen more and more. YHVH is unseating demonic stuff because there are sons that are now saying, "Father, we are framing what needs to happen." And you frame it in the heavens first. Then YHVH positions you to execute justice from the Sanhedrin of heaven and you come from there with papers to destroy the works of the devil, *"For this purpose the Son of God was manifested, that he might destroy the works of the devil"* (1 John 3:8). The framing of the legislator is to destroy the works of the devil. When the Bible says, *"You shall be my witnesses"* (Acts 1:9), it is talking about you having the full testimony of heaven sitting on you. As you speak, you reveal heaven's nature in the earth that is around you. That is how you become a witness. In Christ you and I have absolute creativity and the ability to terra-form, re-form, and create.

Transrelocation

I often walk around the earth. I am talking about trans-relocating. I have been doing it for years now, since the early nineties. (For more teaching on this subject see my MP3 *Transrelocation*). As part of my witness, I really love it when I can walk in a physical fire and pull somebody out and they do not get burnt. I come home with ash on my hands and t-shirt sometimes, it is all good. I love it when I can go into the water, into a car in which someone is drowning, pull them out, bring them to the surface, then go to help the next one in another nation. I really love it when during an earthquake and someone is about to get hit with a steel beam, and you stand there, stop it, and then hold it so they can get out. I love it when you can go into a prison where someone is being tortured and heal them completely in Yeshua's power. This is only the beginning.

I really want to honour the work that Melchizedek has done in working with the Father to bring us to a point where we can begin to express the fullness of YHVH.

You had better believe weird things are starting to happen. YHVH is releasing this on the face of the earth and He has given us the responsibility to engage, go in and go deeper into places you have never been before. Do not worry about anything that is around you. Keep your eyes fixed on the right place and the supply of your source – Yeshua and give your walk in YHVH a framework to be released around your life. And then YHVH will do it for your life.

Activation

Thank you, Father.

Father, today I stand in my position.

Father, today I bless the readers in the name of Yeshua.

Father, I ask that the spark of life, their full framework of the full knowledge of the testimony of YHVH within them, would begin to build to such a point, Father, that the candle will burn all the outer coverings.

Father, I ask that the light of YHVH would begin to flow into their very essence, into their bones, into their DNA.

Father, I ask that You would begin to open up an understanding with Wisdom for them. Father, that as they dwell with Wisdom and participate in functionality with her provision, Father, that You would begin to orchestrate change deep in the hearts of these men and women.

Father, I ask for unusual signs and wonders to become part of their normal life. I ask for the weird. I ask for the unusual, the supernatural occurrences, Father, that we have thought about, and dreamed about and have not thought we would ever see, Father, that those unusual occurrences would begin to become part of their daily life.

Father, I ask for Your glory, and Your love and Your face to be turned towards them. As they walk towards Your faces, that You would make them flawless (Genesis 17:1).

Father, I ask that Your presence would drive them into the wilderness (Hosea 2:14) that we might be able to come out of that place leaning on our Beloved (Song of Songs 8:5).

Father, I bless them. I call them into their inheritance, Father, that the inheritance that knows no bounds, pressed down, shaken out and running over would become their portion (Luke 6:38).

Father, I thank You for the angelic realm and ask that You would unlock it for them. Empower them, Father, to become more and more aware of Your desire towards them to endue them with understanding so they are able to walk into some of these things, Father.

Yeshua, I thank You that You are doing this because You are the Firstborn of many and You are forever a Priest after the Order of Melchizedek. And if You have followed that Order and become part of it Lord, then we would walk into that Order and become part of bringing order, Father, in the name of Yeshua.

Father, I ask for a Father's blessing over these men and women, that the truth of relationship with Your presence, a love affair, Father, would start with Your glory, and with Your Personhood. Lord, that You would make Yourself real, not just to have a thought, but make yourself real and tangibly known to them, Father, in the name of Yeshua.

Jesus, thank You. Holy Spirit, thank You. Thank You, Holy Spirit. You are just amazing. You are so wonderful. Thank You that You are a person and we can have You with us.

Lord, we want to host Your presence. Lord, in the name of Yeshua. Hallelujah.

Chapter 11
The Law of Righteousness

Now we have looked at the amazing call we have in the Order of Melchizedek, made available to us through the blood of Christ, it is important not to feel overwhelmed as if this call is far above us, but to remember that is it all by His righteousness. So I would like to finish this book by looking at that subject.

I became very fascinated with righteousness in my faith walk because all of us want to be righteous and to feel righteous. We want to have that sense of well-being where I feel righteous and I feel holy and I feel fully redeemed before the presence of YHVH. So we set about constructing a whole lot of laws of our own. Things like, I will not do this and I will not do that, and if I do that then I will do this to make me feel better.

Righteousness is a gift that is renewed by YHVH to us each time we enter His realm (1 John 1:9). So the Law of Righteousness is YHVH's capacity where He has opened up the veil to give you and me right of entry to come into the realm of His presence. There He will strip unrighteousness off us as a gift (Romans 3:24). That is the law, right there. It is the power to receive when you are totally unworthy to receive. When you have no foundation for anything to sit on but the gift of His desire towards you to make you clean. That is why Yeshua is called our High Priest. That is why we need to come to our High Priest because Yeshua is the administrator of righteousness. *"Seeing then that we have a great high priest, that is passed into the heavens, Jesus the Son of God, let us hold fast our profession"* (Hebrews 4:14 JK2000).

In the Psalms *"David also describes the blessedness of the man, unto whom God imputes righteousness without works"* (Romans 4:6). The word "impute" means to ascribe or accredit, and I have experienced the Lord doing this – forcefully imputing that right standing into me even when the demonic has another agenda. So it is like putting a seed into hard ground, taking it and pushing it into the ground. So we get blessed when we come into the realm of the presence of YHVH because He strips off our unrighteousness and He purposefully puts righteousness onto us. He cloaks us in righteousness and He houses us in that content. *"Because of God you are ·in [united with; in relationship with] Christ Jesus, who has become for us wisdom from God. ·In Christ we are put right with God, and have been made holy, and have been set free from sin [and became for us righteousness, holiness, and redemption]"* (1 Corinthians 1:30 EXB). So that is the law. The law is, you come in and you become clean (Zechariah 3:4-5). But if you do not come in, you will never become clean. You will try and earn brownie points to make yourself feel clean, to make yourself become clean by living under rules instead of coming in and having your life transformed.

Righteousness is about transforming your life from one thing into another without you being involved in it. It is a gift. That is why Jesus died. This is the gift of the Gospel and the Kingdom to you and I, that we can go in and become clean. It is not the sacrifice's job to make itself clean *"offer your bodies as a living sacrifice"* (Romans 12:1), it is the job of the high priest to make the sacrifice clean. Our job is to go where the high priest is so that He can administrate that through us and inside of us.

In Matthew 6:51 it says this: *"But seek you first the kingdom of God, and his righteousness; and all these things shall be added unto you"* (Matthew 6:33). I want to talk about His righteousness here. This is a very clear statement that I am not to seek my own righteousness but, rather, His. So why then, in religious circles, are there so many laws about trying to become righteous? When you seek His righteousness, it means you have to come into relationship. What happens, then, if I do not seek that righteousness? I try to do it on my own. Therefore I do not need Him and I do not have to relate to Him, and often it is your flesh that will stop you wanting to relate because it wants unrighteousness, being the seed bed for its pleasure, *"Training us to deny ungodliness and worldly desires and to live in a manner that is self-controlled and righteous and godly in the present age"* (Titus 2:12 TLV).

So the Bible says, *"But seek you first the kingdom of God, and his righteousness; and all these things shall be added unto you"* (Matthew 6:33), which is the manifestation of the government of YHVH on the inside – the Kingdom of God is within you. Seek first that governmental manifestation and His righteousness and then all of this is going to be added to you, which is all of that Kingdom. All of this is going to be added to you but it starts with the foundation, which is the government within you.

Engage in that government and then His righteousness will come out of relationship because Yeshua gives it to you totally and absolutely free. It does not matter what you have done, where you have been, the stuff you think that you will never be able to get redeemed from, no matter how much has been done to you or what you have done to others. Even murderers can come into His presence and get totally and absolutely clean and free from every demonic entanglement.

I knew a lady that I worked with in New Zealand who was a foster child, a child of the state because of her parent's issues, and this girl was passed around from home to home. Every home she went into she was abused and by the time she was fourteen she had become a prostitute. Between fourteen and twenty she operated out of prostitution and throughout that time she used to go into this little fantasy world where she would try to escape the pain. There was a being there that looked like her imaginary husband and so she had this little marriage ceremony where she put a ring on her finger to this being, and so this being would help her and look after her and cuddle her in her pain. But by the time she was twenty this demonic being would be waiting for her to abuse her at night time. So the lady came into the conference and, through the conference time, we were working with her and in ministry. I gave her some homework to do about the gateways (see my Gateways of the Three-Fold Nature of Man manual). Before she went away I said to her, *"You need to step into the realm of the presence of YHVH"*. Very often people who are broken know how to do this. She came back six months later a totally different, changed, transformed person, because the gift of YHVH had been given to her to bring her into righteousness. YHVH had removed the record of all the sound inside her body of every single guy she had ever slept with. She had gone through the divorce protocol and taken the ring off her finger, no longer married to that demon spirit, she was able to think for herself for the first time in her life since she was six years old. She was totally healed and delivered in the Lord's gift of righteousness.

I did not spend hours praying with her. I taught her the law of righteousness. Because this law has pre-eminence, it then sets the redemptive process in place for the government of the Kingdom of YHVH to rest in her because the pattern looks like YHVH and YHVH will fill the shadow that looks like Him.

So the Word says, *"Seek first the kingdom of* God" *(Matthew 6:33)* which is the foundation of the government of YHVH. Then it says *"His righteousness"*. It is a very clear statement that it is not your own, not to seek your own righteousness, but rather His. So what does it mean? Let's have a look at the original word in Greek. The word 'righteousness' means 'equity'. It also means 'innocence'[19]. So let's talk about this word equity for a minute because we have a lot of arguments about equality and wanting to be equal in our modern culture. So that is why it says about Jesus *"Christ Jesus: Who, being in the form of God, thought it not a thing to be grasped to be equal with God: But made himself of no reputation, and took upon him the form of a servant, and was made in the likeness of men"* (Philippians 2:5-7).

So, let us talk about this issue of equity.To come in to equity

---

[19] The Greek word for righteousness is described in Strong's Bible Dictionary as "equitable (in character or act) and by implication innocent, holy (absolutely or relatively), just, meet, right(eous)" (1342).

means to be given the opportunity to have the same standing as something. So what that means is, if I am going to have a fight with my sister here, giving her equity means having one arm tied behind my back and both my feet tied together because my physical body is stronger than hers. Giving someone equity means putting them on a right standing to have the same power as I have, the same influence, the same protocol and the same opportunities. When we give equity to someone, it brings them into equality and makes them become equal.

Yeshua has come in and given us His righteousness, giving us the ability to become equal with Him because He is the first born of many. He then brings us into equality to become sons, *"...whom he did foreknow, he also did predestinate to be conformed to the image of his Son, that he might be the firstborn among many brethren"* (Romans 8:29). Now, I am not saying I am equal with Jesus, but this is what righteousness does. It is because it comes as a gift. So when righteousness comes, you actually stand in the same standing as Christ, totally and absolutely righteous. Can you see how YHVH works in this? So YHVH is wanting to release the Kingdom Realm and He is looking for a platform but it is based out of the Kingdom, becoming righteous and then everything else is going to be added.

You cannot express the Kingdom properly through your life until you grasp the importance of the role of righteousness within you and within your life. Both righteousness and equity go hand in hand. Without one you cannot appreciate the other. Without being given equity, you cannot appreciate righteousness, and without righteousness you cannot appreciate equity. Equity means I have got enough to pay for everything I need to have done.

The words are "seek first the Kingdom of YHVH". So the words 'seek first' mean to 'diligently look to obtain'. It means to make a high priority of that in your life. So your highest priority is spending time to engage the Kingdom. I have helpful triggers all around myself. My car door is a trigger for me to step into the Realm of the Kingdom and close myself into it. My shower door is a trigger to go through the shower door and close the shower door and stand in the presence of YHVH. At the dinner table, from the moment I sit down, it is a trigger to sit down at the table of the presence of YHVH. Opening my front door is a trigger to step out into the Realm of the Kingdom when I go into the world. I have triggers like this all around my life that I use to continually engage me in the realm of the presence of YHVH so they can bring me into the place of standing in equity all day. To use those kinds of things as triggers engages the Kingdom to sit around your life, to facilitate through you the expression of YHVH in the world around you.

Righteousness produces holiness which is not that I am cleaner than you. It means 'looking into revelation and going wow!' It produces revelation ,which creates holiness and produces the glory of YHVH inside of you. It releases and produces the tangible reality of YHVH through you onto the earth today.

There are three things that righteousness does. That is the first one. The second one is, righteousness sanctifies and adjusts your behavioural patterns and desires that dwell within you. So, when you have issues, or you are struggling with stuff inside your life, you need to step into the realm of the presence of YHVH and engage His righteousness because doing that changes the record of this. So instead of going down the pathway of engaging sin and feeling guilty, which is the normal process, the moment you find yourself going down that pathway, it can be anywhere, even right to the very end expression of your sin, you still have the capacity to step in and engage. That, alone, will begin to change this record. It is a continual thing, so if you find you are struggling with sin, step in. It does not matter if it is seven hundred and ninety-five times a day. Step into the realm of the presence of YHVH and engage righteousness. This will change the record of sin because stepping into His presence gives you equity to override the sin.

The third thing that righteousness does is to restore innocence. This destroys the enemy's access to your life. When YHVH gives you innocence, the enemy cannot enter that innocence because there is no pollution in it. So when you step into the realm of the presence of YHVH, the law of righteousness activates and you engage His righteousness. This is because Jesus gives righteousness to you and you receive it by faith. When you step out into His presence, it brings you into the realm of imputed innocence. The enemy has to try and pollute innocence again. The moment I feel the battle, I step in, using that pressure as a driving point to engage me to step into the realm of His presence. So I stay there on a continual basis, as best as I can. When I am not there and this stuff starts, I say "thank you Yeshua", that is my door: my trigger is, when this starts, I step in.

Righteousness has its basis in three things. The first one is that it joins us to the person of YHVH. *"But he that is joined unto the Lord is one spirit"* (1 Corinthians 6:17). Righteousness joins us to the presence of YHVH. It actually connects us umbilically with the provision of Heaven on the earth.

Righteousness is a gift that is given to us and righteousness is one part of the armour. I do a teaching called armoured for battle (on MP3 available on my website), which is not dealing with 'the helmet of salvation, breastplate of righteousness, belt of truth, etc.' A parrot can do that and that is, unfortunately, what the church has done because they do not understand that this is for the evil day. *"Therefore take unto you the whole armor of God, that you may be able to withstand in the evil day, and having done all, to stand"* (Ephesians 6:13). The evil day is when the visitation of YHVH's glory is on the face of the earth where judgement happens. It is not for today. If you are not carrying that revelation and walking it out, it will not be yours anyway, so it is no good repeating the words like a parrot. It does not do a thing for you.

Righteousness is armour that you receive out of the presence of YHVH and you actually have to put over your life. When you go in there, you receive righteousness as an armour that comes around you so that you can destroy the works of the enemy with it because the enemy's work is unrighteousness. Righteousness will destroy unrighteousness because it changes the record of unrighteousness and makes it righteous.

Righteousness itself has its very basis in the character and actual nature of the person of YHVH. *"And Jesus said unto him, Why call me good? There is none good but one, that is, God"* (Mark 10:18). Just like a man and woman become one flesh when married through sexual union with one another, righteousness becomes a very cord and tie between you and the person of YHVH in union. "But the one who is united *and* joined to the Lord is one spirit *with Him" (1 Corinthians 6:17 AMP).* Righteousness is the soul tie between you and the presence of YHVH. So, if I want to be soul tied to the presence of YHVH, it comes through that righteousness. This is your soul tie to the presence of YHVH and how to get joined to Him in righteousness. Because there is none like Him and I want to become like Him.

To be soul tied in righteousness to the presence of YHVH is to be vitally connected to Him in the Realm of His presence in all that we do. So, in everything that I am doing, I am connected to that whole realm with His righteousness facilitating through my life and around me. We are supposed to function out of that Realm here, on the face of the earth.

If you are joined to someone, you get joined to their character, to their nature and you are influenced by them in everything that you do. One of the most exciting things about this gift of righteousness is that where you are, YHVH is also. So when you are here, you are with Him because you are joined to His presence. So where you go, He goes. Where you move, He moves. It is sonship and relationship, but you are not supposed to move until He moves. So when He moves and goes, you can move and go. *"Therefore Yeshua answered them, "Amen, amen I tell you, the Son cannot do anything by Himself. He can do only what He sees the Father doing. Whatever the Father does, the Son does likewise"* (John 5:19 TLV).Yeshua went in and engaged and saw and moved with the Father while He was down here. Hallelujah! Righteousness engages you in the movement of YHVH.

Righteousness is imputed and it is a gift. (Romans *4:6, 11).* Impute means 'to be charged with' or 'to ascribe to'.*(James 2:23)*

It is a process and a progress. We must believe that it is imputed when we are called friends of YHVH because it requires you to believe. It requires you to believe, then righteousness is given and you are called sons of YHVH. Without this righteousness you will never be called a son of YHVH. We receive this righteous as we go into His presence and engage it and allow Him to cloak it around us. The moment you get cloaked, you become a son. There are three simple steps:

1) Believe
2) Allow the imputation to happen
3) Allow Him to call you friend.

"Enoch walked with God: and he was not; for God took him" (Genesis 5:24). Friend! So if you do not want to die, become a friend because, when you are a friend, that will change you here.

Righteousness is a gift, that is true as the Bible says, "…A man is not justified by the works of the law, but by the faith of Jesus Christ…" (Galatians 2:16), and in Christ "we have redemption through his blood, the forgiveness of sins, according to the riches of his grace" (Ephesians 1:7). But if the full provision was automatically empowered in our lives without our having to do anything then Paul would not have written, *"But I roughly treat my body, and bring it into subjection: lest that by any means, when I have preached to others, I myself should be disqualified"* (1 Corinthians 9:27). So it is true that it has been done. We *"are set right as a gift of His grace, through the redemption that is in Messiah Yeshua"* (Romans 3:24 TLV). The issue is, that it is not the whole truth because this gift, truth, has to be outworked in your life and there are protocols to outwork it in your life. There is a religious spirit that actually does not want to crucify flesh as the Word tells us, *"Those who belong to Christ Jesus have crucified ·their own sinful selves [the sinful nature; the flesh]. They have given up ·their old selfish feelings and the evil things they wanted to do [its passions and desires]"* (Galatians 5:24 EXB). That religious spirit does not want to take responsibility for the issues in your life but just say *"Oh Jesus has done it all"*. Jesus

has given you provision to action it all, but you and I have got to appropriate it to our lives.

Yeshua's death on the cross destroyed the power of sin but we must deal with the desires of sin. Yes, Yeshua has destroyed the power of it, but we have got to deal with the desire of it, which is appropriating that down here in its fullness. Righteousness cannot be earned by fervent righteous practices of law to stop you sinning. People say to me "Oh Ian, I have got control of that issue in my life now". Well that is really great, actually control is not the issue. The issue is, is it dead? Because anything that is in control will eventually come out and manifest again. It has to be dead. That is the real issue.

It is a gift given to us by Jesus when He hung on the cross *(Isaiah 53)*. The cross is a place of exchange. When He died He took all that we have done, all that we are doing and all that we ever will do in exchange, where His righteousness becomes ours. The key to this exchange is your willingness to allow Him to carry it. You have got to be willing for Jesus to carry your rubbish. But the problem is, most of us are not willing because we want to have a sense of control, that we have done something to make ourselves feel better so that we feel like we have achieved something. But righteousness is not about you. The Law of Righteousness has nothing to do with you, it is all about Him. So you step into that and the Law has precedence over your stuff which is sin and death. The Law of Righteousness has the precedence over the Law of Sin & Death, which releases the Law of the Spirit of Life and leads to the Law of Faith. So you have all these things working together, forming a house for the presence of YHVH to come and live in. It is exciting to me – this is an exciting faith walk!

"No weapon that is formed against you shall prosper; and every tongue that shall rise against you in judgment you shall condemn. This is the heritage of the servants of the LORD, and their righteousness is of me, says the LORD" (Isaiah 54:17*)*. *"By the word of truth, by the power of God, by the armor of righteousness..."* (2 Corinthians 6:7). It means we have weapons of war. The primary purpose of the armour of

righteousness is for defence because the devil cannot penetrate righteousness.

But our own righteousness is different: "…All our righteousness's are as filthy rags" (Isaiah 64:6). That means every time you have said, *"I will not do this today, and make myself feel better"* It is just a filthy rag you have just put on yourself. So instead of carrying the garment of righteousness, you are carrying a filthy rag which will smell differently to a garment. Anything that carries a different fragrance from the right garment attracts different things to it. So if you have a lot of stuff that has been attracted to you, it may be because of the rubbish that you have been engaging in because you are trying to earn righteousness. Every time you try and earn righteousness by living a set of man-made laws in your life, you attract the demonic to yourself because you smell like filthy rags in the spirit realm.

So, how do we engage this truth? The first thing is to acknowledge that 'I am trying to do it myself'. Simply, *"YHVH, I have sinned"* Have you have ever said that? We need to acknowledge it by repenting for trying to earn righteousness and for having been self-righteous and rejecting the gift of the offering that Yeshua has given to us. We need to actually repent for rejecting the gift of righteousness that Yeshua has given us in wanting to do it our way. This is something that we need to walk through on a continual basis inside our lives.

We need to receive His righteouness by faith. It helps to dream about what that means. I have spent hours at my desk, by my computer or driving my car thinking about *'man, I wonder what it is going to be like to actually have that whole thing totally manifested so that I am totally righteous in all and everything, in every detail of my life. I wonder what that is going to be like?'* I allow myself to think about those kind of things because it empowers me to dream about the potential possibility of what it can be like to be absolutely and totally free. To be totally free from the empowerment of things that go on around us and to facilitate the desire of YHVH inside the middle of what we are doing. You will raise a standard by doing that and it will roar inside your spirit manand raising the standard is important.

We also need to be thankful – "Lord thank You that You have given me all righteousness, You have given it to me as a free gift. *Lord I am so thankful that you have given me this. Lord I am so grateful that you have empowered me and you have opened the veil so that I can come through that veil and stand and receive from you Lord. I am so thankful that you have given me the power to stand in righteousness, stand in truth and stand under the power."* I do that on a continual basis.

There is a circle. I call it the circle of life that governs the Law of Righteousness, that goes;acknowledge, repent, receive, restore, reveal. Acknowledge, repent, receive, restore, reveal. Four R's. It is amazing when you understand a building and how builders make a building. They set a corner stone. That is why Yeshua is called the corner stone. Corner Stone actually means 'one with a bent knee'. So you understand an apostolic government by the bent knee, not by having many people connected to your network. It is about your bent knee. Then the foundation needs four corner stones on it to make the building totally square but they are all set off one. So you have the four corner stones and then you have a door. Your doorway of entry and the doorway out of you is righteousness. Nothing will flow out of you unless righteousness is properly established. Nothing will function through you and your ability to go in unless there is righteousness. So you go in and become a door, going in and out all day every day, walking out the process.

My big question to you today is *"Where are you?"* YHVH is calling us to receive His Kingdom and that Kingdom exists in righteousness. YHVH is holding out a gift to you today saying, *"Here is my righteousness. Will you be prepared to receive it? All you have to do is come into my presence and you can receive it"*. That is all you have to do. Let's practise doing that today. So I would like you to stand on your feet and find a place that you can take a step forward. Thank you Holy Spirit. Hallelujah!

Activation

Close your eyes and take a small step forward.

Father, according to Your word, You tore the veil. You sent

Your Son to die on the cross, to have total victory over the enemy, to open a way of escape for me, to open a doorway into the realm of Your presence, to be able to obtain all that You have given to me, all the provision that You laid up for me in treasures in heaven. Lord, I want to acknowledge, today, that I have sinned by rejecting the gift of Your righteousness. I acknowledge, today, Lord, that I have tried to do it my way. I have lived my life by a set of laws that have governed me and controlled my life where I have tried to control issues of brokenness and sinfulness in my life. I want to acknowledge, Lord, that I have done this my way. Lord, today, I want to repent freely and acknowledge this freely before you and before the angels of YHVH that are in heaven.

Lord, we stand and we repent today in the name of Yeshua. Lord, I thank You that You have made a way for me to receive from You and that it is by entering into the realm of Your presence. Father, Your Word says that Joshua was a High Priest and that you have called us a Kingdom of Priests. You have called us Kings and Priests of YHVH and Father, today, I want to come in that role of a priest Lord, and by faith, today, I want to step in to the realm of Your presence and I do that by my body (take a step forward). Father, I step into the realm of Your presence. Today Lord, I stand in this realm and, according to Your Word, the first thing You look at when satan stands to acuse me of unrighteousness, the first thing You look at is a filthy garment and, Lord, the first thing you say is "remove the filthy garment from their life and cloak them with a new garment."

Father, today, I acknowledge that that garment is the garment of righteousness, the pure linen garment of Your presence. Yeshua HaMashiach, I exchange my garment of unrighteousness for the garment of righteousness that You give me as a free gift. Lord, today, I put that over my body and my soul and my spirit and it becomes a covering for who I am in You, in relationship. Yeshua, I receive Your gift today, freely and willingly. I set my desire, Lord, that I receive this from You today. Lord, I know that I cannot earn this but this is a gift You have given me and I receive it willingly today.

Lord, I want to be tied and joined to You and joining comes through righteousness and Lord, I thank You today that I am joined to Your presence. Father, I receive that from You today, destroying everything that is unrighteous in my life. Father, today, as I step back into this world, I bring the garment of the righteousness of YHVH back into the atmosphere of this world. Father, I carry this garment over my body, over my life. Lord, I display it in this realm of the earth, into everything that is in darkness. I display the garment of righteousness that I now carry because my Father has imputed to me righteousness and given me a garment, holy, unblemished and spotless and I stand in the revelation of that today, Father, in this world and allow it to be seen that I stand righteously before my Lord and my King. Yeshua, I thank You that you have removed from me all unrighteousness. You have removed from me all record of sin and I stand in this garment of righteousness as if I have never sinned.

Father, I thank You for the blood of Yeshua that has made a way for me to stand in this today. Lord, I receive it. I ask that You empower me to administrate on the face of the earth where I walk, what I do, what I say, what I see, what I hear, Father, so that the expression of Your Kingdom would come out of this righteousness by power of Holy Spirit in the Name of Yeshua HaMashiach. Amen

About Ian

Ian Clayton is the founder of Son of Thunder Ministries and passionately pursues a life of understanding and getting to know who the person of God really is.

Ian travels itinerantly by invitation throughout New Zealand, Africa, America, Europe and Asia ministering, teaching, equipping and mandating people to become sons of God.

Ian's heart in founding Son of Thunder is to have an avenue to put strategies and keys into believers' hands to enable them to actively participate in the reality of the realms of God's Kingdom and to experience the empowerment of life as the spirit beings we were created to be.

Ian trains and equips believers to give their lives in a persistent, passionate pursuit of the person of God, enabling them to discover that their lives are about the preparation for oneness and unity with God for the purpose of becoming mandated and authorised ambassadors of His Kingdom. His passion is to reveal to the sons of God the purpose of the power of the attorney of God within them, removing the sense of powerlessness and hopelessness that is often attached to many in the body of Christ when they are confronted with the reality of the spirit world that surrounds them.

www.sonofthunder.org

Published by
Son of Thunder Publications

www.sonofthunderpublications.org

Made in the USA
Middletown, DE
22 May 2021